Coping with Poverty

Pentecostals and

Christian Base

Communities

in Brazil

Coping with Poverty

Cecília Loreto Mariz

 Temple University Press
Philadelphia

Temple University Press, Philadelphia 19122

⊗ The paper used in this publication meets the minimum
requirements of American National Standard for Information
Sciences—Permanence of Paper for Printed Library Materials,
ANSI Z39.48-1984

Library of Congress Cataloging-in-Publication Data
Mariz, Cecília Loreto.
    Coping with poverty : Pentecostals and Christian base
communities in Brazil / Cecília Loreto Mariz.
        p.   cm.
    Includes bibliographical references and index.
    ISBN 1-56639-112-1 (alk. paper).—ISBN 1-56639-113-X (pbk. :
alk. paper)
    1. Pentecostal churches—Brazil. 2. Basic Christian
communities—Brazil. 3. Brazil—Religious life. 4. Poverty—
Research—Brazil. 5. Poverty—Religious aspects—Christianity.
I. Title.
    BX8762.A45B66   1994
    289.9'4'0981—dc20   93-12511

FOR MY PARENTS,

Geraldo Mariz and Maria Hilda Loreto Mariz

CONTENTS

ACKNOWLEDGMENTS

I am indebted to the Universidade Federal de Pernambuco and to the Conselho de Aperfeicoamento de Pessoal de Ensino Superior (CAPES) for supporting my stay at Boston University, where I wrote the first version of this book. At Boston University, I was helped by many professors. I cannot mention all of them, but I would like to thank Peter Berger and Paule Verdet. Dr. Berger offered me not only a strong intellectual stimulus but also the facilities of the Institute for the Study of the Economic Culture.

I wrote the present version of this book in Brazil, and I would not have been able to do so without the help of many people. Dean Graber and Kristine Stenzel helped me in editing the text. Dean Graber also offered me valuable assistance with his comments, encouragement, and friendship. I am very grateful to them and to many other colleagues, among them Roberto Motta, Rubem César Fernandes, and Maria da Dores Campos Machado, whose comments and criticism helped in rewriting and updating the whole work.

I would like to thank Doris Braendel and Heidi Trombert of Temple University Press for their careful editorial guidance.

Finally, I also thank all the interviewees for being so friendly and for having made my field research very pleasant.

Coping with Poverty

INTRODUCTION

The recent growth of Protestantism in Latin America has attracted the attention of intellectuals and the media and has stimulated debate about the meaning and consequences of this religious phenomenon. Some observers view the "Protestantization" of Latin America negatively—a result of U.S. imperialism (Lima 1988); others predict that a larger population of Protestants will bring positive changes to the region, creating a more modern, democratic society (Martin 1990). Along with Guatemala and Chile, Brazil is mentioned as a good example of this surge of Protestantism (Stoll 1990). According to the Censo Institucional Evangélico (Institutional Evangelical Census) carried out in 1992 (Fernandes 1992), in the Rio de Janeiro metropolitan area one new Protestant church is opened every two days.

Religion is entrenched in the everyday lives of its practitioners and has a deep affinity with the psychological experiences that result from their material needs and activities. Economic conditions and material lifestyles have direct consequences for the beliefs people adopt. To understand the meaning of the religious changes taking place in Latin America, one must see them within their cultural and economic contexts. By this, I do not mean to suggest that religion is economically determined but that it is important to understand the material conditions of people's lives in order to understand their beliefs.

MACRO AND MICRO
APPROACHES TO POVERTY

Certainly Brazilians from all social strata experience religious changes, but considering the size of the poor population in Brazil, poverty becomes a fundamental element in understanding the changes taking place in the Brazilian religious arena. The most pressing problem in Brazilian society is poverty. More than half the Brazilian population lives in a very precarious situation that varies from simple poverty to total misery (Jaguaribe et al. 1986). The proliferation of shantytowns, beggars, and abandoned street children in the urban areas is the concrete expression of this poverty. Social indicators such as life expectancy and infant mortality are its statistical expression.[1]

Despite all the changes Brazilian society has undergone and the economic growth that has characterized Brazil during the second half of the twentieth century, poverty persists. Industrialization and modernization have not fulfilled their potential for overcoming poverty. Indeed, there is a striking contrast between Brazilian social indicators and its economic growth and national product. Despite having the world's eleventh largest gross national income (GNI), Brazil presents social indicators similar to those of the poor countries in Africa (Jaguaribe et al. 1986; Valle Silva 1991). Comparing the Human Development Index (HDI), an index of life quality, of 160 countries, a 1990 United Nations Development Program report ranked Brazil sixty-second. This enormous gap between economic growth and quality of life may, at first, be explained by the size of Brazil's population. As a matter of fact, when the per capita GNI of different countries is compared, Brazil is ranked sixtieth and not eleventh (Faria 1991). Nevertheless, this report concludes that "the disparity among countries is much greater in income than in human development"—that is, factors other than economic wealth play a role in determining people's quality of life (Faria 1991).

Recent Brazilian history underlines this fact. During the 1970s, Brazil experienced a remarkable economic growth that was known as the "Brazilian miracle" (Jaguaribe et al. 1989). But this growth, though it was a necessary condition to improve living standards in the country, by itself proved insufficient to eliminate misery and improve the quality of life for most of the population. In contrast, during the 1980s—considered by Brazilian economists the "lost decade" because of the economic crisis and the decrease in GNI and personal income—social indicators did not become worse; paradoxically, they even underwent a slight improvement (Faria 1991). The 1980s in Brazil was a decade of redemocratization, or *Abertura*, characterized by such political changes as the reestablishment of democracy and the flourishing of social movements.

Vilmar Faria suggests a relation between life-quality indicators and the organization of people into social movements.[2] In fact, life-quality indicators, such as the infant mortality rate, life expectancy, and the literacy rate, depend not only on economic resources and the political distribution of these resources but also on the adoption of new attitudes and values by the population. The value placed on education and the demand for more hygienic housing conditions, for example, play an important role in determining life quality. Economic and political transformations affect culture, but they do not determine it. They also depend on specific cultural conditions in order to be actualized.[3] Compared with economic and technological changes, cultural transformations move at a slower pace and escape the control of social planners, economists, and politicians. They depend less on macrosocial educational policies or nationwide political programs and more on grassroots activities. Perhaps for those reasons, they have been underestimated.

Poverty is a multidimensional problem. Despite its roots in the social-class structure and its relation to international and national economic and political contexts, poverty is experienced as a personal problem and can be combated at a personal–

familial level (Clark 1988). That is, the struggle against poverty occurs not only at the macrosocial level of economic and political governmental decisions but also at the microsocial level of poor people's organizations and families. The macro perspective views poverty in relation to the social structure. From this perspective, poverty is quantifiably defined from the standpoint of the outsider. At the macro level, social scientists and planners use statistical data, such as a decrease in the infant mortality rate, to measure the efficacy of proposed solutions.

The micro approach stresses the standpoint of the poor themselves, whose poverty is an everyday experience. Micro-level actions have limited, immediate, and specific goals. For example, poor people attempt to solve the water-supply problem in their neighborhood or try to increase their incomes. The life opportunities of a poor individual thus do not entirely depend on the structural elements of the whole society. Factors such as the organizational and cultural attitudes of the poor may help to overcome a specific material problem or more general ones. Although more limited in their consequences than larger political measures, these everyday attempts to improve living conditions by small groups of the poor and their families are equally important. The everyday struggles of the poor may not only solve an immediate need, allowing a particular population to survive, but may also foster cultural transformations, producing a long-standing and less reversible change in the population.

In affirming the importance of microsocial factors, it is not my intention to dismiss the social causes of poverty or to foster the belief that individuals are independent from society. Instead, my aim is simply to recognize other dimensions of poverty and to acknowledge that social structure can also be a result of, and can be affected by, the actions of organized individuals. In essence, to affirm this point is to attempt to avoid a reification of the social structure. In this perspective, therefore, individuals' lives are not seen as completely socially determined and human beings are not reduced to consequences of social structure; they are also seen as the constructors of reality. That is, there is "a dialectical relation between the structural realities and the human enterprise of constructing reality—in history" (Berger and Luckmann 1966, 186). In other words, despite being limited by society, individuals can at times supersede and change society. Such actions and changes are not performed by isolated individuals, however, but by individuals as members of groups, within which shared values and ideas are developed and actualized as a social reality. Accordingly, poor people are not helpless; they can and do act in order to change their situations.

Too often underestimated, the poor have the potential to be agents of social transformation. Unfortunately, the idea that the poor are guilty of causing their own poverty is widely held by social scientists. Some social scientists even hold an opposite and equally erroneous opinion that individuals are the powerless victims of social structure. This belief that the poor are completely powerless and can do nothing to improve their lives is nearly as harmful as blaming them for their poverty.

Micro and macro social transformations are not isolated phenomena. Small groups encourage individual changes, and when these changes are deeply felt, they can foster a qualitative transformation of the social structure. An analysis from the micro standpoint, which tries to avoid a mechanistic analysis that perceives people's actions as a direct consequence of macrosocial factors, takes into account the cultural meaning people ascribe to their actions. In addition, the cultural approach prevents us from perceiving actions as merely the result of individual decisions (Page 1984) and helps us see them as a result of their social construction.

RELIGION AND MICROSOCIAL
COPING STRATEGIES

Cultural changes fostered by small groups may help the poor cope with poverty or even escape from it. It is impossible to deny the importance of culture in fostering motivation and offering symbolic conditions for social change.[4] But to stress the importance of cultural factors and cultural changes in the process of overcoming poverty does not assume that poverty has cultural causes or that poverty is a cultural problem.[5] Theories that blame the culture of the poor for their deprivation or for the absence of social changes occur throughout the study of Third World countries, in very different sociological perspectives. Modernization theories, for example, relate poverty to the culture of a particular poor people, blaming their traditions for the underdevelopment of their country. And Marxism sees poor people from the Third World as alienated and unable to transform their society. Both views are ethnocentric (Berger 1974).

Religion is an important part of any culture, and in Brazilian culture, religion is even more important than in most societies. Thus, to understand Brazilian culture means to understand Brazil's religious landscape and how it relates to Brazilian society. Recent changes in the religious life of the Brazilian poor have greatly affected both their lifestyle and their culture in general. They have, therefore, affected the microsocial strategies people develop to cope with poverty.

In Marx's (1957) thought, religion is the opiate of the masses, the veil that hides the truth of class exploitation, preventing the poor from changing society. Social change requires true class consciousness, which is possible only through a politically critical and rational interpretation of society. Because Marx considered all religions equally deprived of rational qualities and in opposition to rational thought, for him religion could never help humans free themselves from social or material oppression; consequently, religion could never help the poor. Instead, religion was an instrument for the political oppression of the poorest. Marxist-oriented studies about religions are concerned with an ideological critique of their beliefs and worldviews.

Ideological critiques and the historical materialist concepts of "alienation" and "false consciousness," however, do not take into account the standpoint of the poor, and thus they limit our ability to understand the reasons for the popularity of religion among the poor. Rather than define religions in terms of the degree to which they alienate people from their class interests, it is more helpful to understand the popularity of religion by analyzing how each religious practice and belief affects the everyday lives of people. In fact, the religious beliefs of the poor may have utilitarian value in the quotidian and may not be a mere "illusory solution" to economic problems and social crisis (Hurbon 1986).

The Weberian approach, which tries to understand how religion can ascribe meaning to economic activities, is more helpful for our purpose than the Marxist approach. In his *The Protestant Ethic and the Spirit of Capitalism*, Weber (1948) shows how Protestantism ascribed meaning to materially instrumental behavior that fostered capitalist and industrialized society. Weber sees rational knowledge and behavior as useful for survival in capitalist society. Despite Marx's and Weber's different interpretations of the modern world and capitalist society, both share the idea that the substitution of reason for myth helps the poor to solve their problems. For Weber, however, there are degrees of rationalization, and the process of rationalization occurs not only within religions but emerges and is spread through religions. Although the core of religion is nonrational, religion can be a "carrier" of rationalization. And, in fact, Weber attempts to show that rationalized religions can help people adopt rational attitudes that in material terms correspond to a capitalist attitude and can lead to affluence. While acknowledging the material superiority and advantages of rational action, however, he remains suspicious of the moral superiority of rational knowledge. And while both Weber and Marx agree that the rationalization of poor people's views helps them in their everyday fight for survival, Marx emphasizes the political power of a rational view, while Weber sees the economic utility of rational behavior.

This book argues that although Brazil's religious groups cling to magical elements, most have tended to develop ethics and a system of theoretical beliefs and have replaced their oral tradition with a written one. This trend is what Weber calls the "rationalization" of religion, in part the result of a broad process of social change, and results in the disappearance of magic and a shift in emphasis from rituals and icons to ethics and responsibilities. The growth of Pentecostalism among the Brazilian poor seems to be part of this trend toward a broad cultural and religious rationalization that occurs also within the Catholic church and in the Afro-Brazilian Spiritist tradition. When the Brazilian poor go to a Pentecostal church, they are not looking for an enchanted religion with magic, miracles, and emotion, as perhaps middle-class people do, because they already have had magic, miracles, and emotion in their previous religions. It seems that the relative rationalization of the Pentecostal worldview is most appealing for the poor. Although it does not imply that emotion, magical elements, and rituals are decreasing or being suppressed, Pentecostalism is still rationalizing, since it introduces a universal ethic and stresses individual choice of religion, exclusivity of religious identity, and the construction of a theoretical system that integrates religious beliefs. This trend is related to the industrialization and modernization of Brazilian society, which has become increasingly global in its values and attitudes. But it also reflects the reaction of the poor, who are trying to control these changes and create a better life for themselves and their families.

To relate religion to material survival does not mean to adopt a functionalist approach to religion, reducing it to a mere economic function. On the contrary, economic life, especially the struggle for survival and the improvement of social conditions, needs to have a meaning. Understanding the meaning of religious practices and beliefs is fundamental because the material consequences of religion in people's everyday lives depend on the meanings their religion carries for them.

In order to understand the meaning of poor people's actions, we must stand in their shoes and see, from their perspective, what it means to live in poverty, what it means to attempt to change conditions, and what religious meaning people ascribe to these strategies of survival. To adopt this view is not to deny the macrosocial elements and causes of poverty, but to analyze the poverty from a different perspective. My intention here is to approach poverty from the microsocial perspective, that is, from the standpoint of the families and organizations of the poor, and to show how their coping with poverty relates to grassroots organization and cultural changes fostered by religion. This book focuses on the everyday struggle for survival inasmuch as this struggle has consequences beyond those of simple survival, and it attempts to identify the transcendent and often unintended consequences of these limited goals, the seeds for broad transformations and their potentialities for macro changes. It attempts to identify the influence of religion in the way people deal with poverty and to understand aspects of the religious transformations in Brazil and to see if the popularity of each religion in Brazil depends on the adequacy of the supports each religion offers its population.

Because Pentecostal Protestant growth in Brazil is part of a broad process of religious and social change, its understanding requires not only an analysis of the Brazilian religious field as a whole but also a comparison of Pentecostals' life experiences with those of people from other religions. In order to compare the different religions of the Brazilian poor and their strategies for coping with poverty I used different kinds of data. My conclusions are based on secondary sources combined with interviews and life histories of members and leaders of each religious group, observations of meetings, and the reading of the religious literature used by each group. The field research took place in the northeastern state of Pernambuco, mainly in poor neighborhoods of Recife, especially in Alto José do Pinho e Alto dos Carneiros and in the Recife metropolitan area, and in the southeastern state of Rio de Janeiro in *favela* areas of the city of Rio de Janeiro, such as Penha, Morro dos Cabritos, and Jacarezinho, as well as in other areas of the state.

CHAPTER I

Religion in Brazil

Brazil is known as a quintessentially Catholic country. As the historian Riolando Azzi reminds us, the Brazilian equivalent of the Statue of Liberty in New York City is the statue of Christ the Redeemer, built by the Catholic church on the Corcovado mountain overlooking the city of Rio de Janeiro. Consequently, it is not possible to understand any change in the religious situation in Brazil without taking into account what is happening within the Catholic church.

THE CATHOLIC CHURCH
IN BRAZIL

In 1990 a Gallup survey about religious options in Brazil showed that Catholics accounted for 76.2 percent of the total population (Carneiro and Soares 1992); in 1980, according to Brazil's census, they were 88.45 percent. Although the percentage has declined dramatically, it is still very high. Viewed by itself, the statistic does not paint a clear picture of the actual situation and may distort reality unless some important aspects of Brazilian history and culture are considered.

These percentages indicate the strength of Catholicism, rather than that of the official Catholic church. The distinction between Catholicism and the Catholic church is very useful in understanding the religious experience in Brazil (Hoornaert 1988). Catholicism is a broad religious phenomenon that can be independent of the Roman Catholic church's official orientation. Although the Catholic church has never been able to embody all the religious experiences of the Brazilian population, especially those of economically deprived people, Brazilians are immersed in the Catholic worldview. Catholicism has provided the language and the theoretical framework that integrate religious elements from several different traditions (Hoornaert 1988). It became the dominant religion in Brazil because it blended and incorporated African and indigenous religions. The hegemony of Catholicism in the Gallup survey and in the census does not represent the hegemony of the Roman Catholic church but that of an old form of Iberian Catholicism that escaped Roman control and mixed with African and indigenous traditions.

The Catholic church's true weakness is revealed in data on attendance at Mass and on surveys of people who intend to choose religious careers. About 20 percent of the Catholic population attends Mass weekly (Antoniazzi 1989).[1] In addition, Brazil has a very high ratio of inhabitants to priests. In

1970, 40.6 percent of all Brazilian priests were foreigners, and there was one priest for every 7,151 inhabitants in Brazil. This ratio grew to one priest for every 9,367 in 1980 and to 10,136 in 1991, while the proportion of foreign priests diminished: Foreigners constituted 38.5 percent in 1980 and 26.5 percent in 1991 of the priests who worked in Brazil, according to data collected by the *Centro de Estatistica Religiosa e Investigação Social* (Center for Religious Statistics and Social Investigation, or CERIS). Referring to the 1980 CERIS data, the situation was better in the southernmost state of Rio Grande do Sul (5,401 inhabitants per priest) and worse in the Northeast (18,500 inhabitants per priest). Moreover, a study by Antônio Flávio Pierucci (1987) about the social origins of priests showed that the highest number of Brazilians who aspired to be priests came from areas where a significant portion of the population had a recent European background, such as the southern states of Paraná and Rio Grande do Sul, where many in the population are descendants of Polish, German, and Italian immigrants. By contrast, the lowest rates of aspiring priests were in northern and northeastern states, where the inhabitants generally do not have a recent European background. It is interesting to note that well-known priests such as Leonardo Boff, Don Vicente Scherer, and Cardeal Lorsheider are all of German descent. In the areas I researched in Recife almost all the priests interviewed were foreigners. This absence of sacerdotal vocation may reveal the distance of Brazilian culture and the majority of the Brazilian population from Roman spiritual patterns. For the Catholic church, Brazil, the largest Catholic nation in the world, is still a mission outpost.[2]

Despite its strong economic and political role, the official Catholic church has had long-standing difficulties being accepted by a large part of the Brazilian population. Brazilian Catholicism was more Portuguese than Roman, and the Catholic church in Brazil had a large degree of autonomy from Rome until about 1850. At that time, the Roman Catholic church began to express concern about its control over the church abroad. Rome's ensuing attempt to unify Catholicism and enhance Roman control over the church worldwide is known as *romanization*. The romanization was also a process of rational reorganization of the Catholic religious field, in which the mind, reason, and logic took priority over myth, emotion, and the body (Hoornaert 1988). This process can be identified with the modern rationalization, in the Weberian sense, of the Catholic church. Therefore, the romanization process can be viewed as part of an internal rationalization of the Catholic church. It indicates a modern bureaucratization and centralization in the Roman church.

For Brazil, the romanization process can be understood as part of a broad process of cultural integration of Brazilian society in the modern international world (Della Cava 1970). The Catholic church, as the largest transnational institution in Brazil, can be considered the major ideological and cultural link between Brazil and modern European societies.

Romanization in Brazil began with the removal of the power of the *Irmandades* (lay fraternities or religious orders). By the middle of the twentieth century, romanization had reached all the clergy, but it never completely took hold among lay people.[3] People affected by the romanization process were mostly from the urban middle class. The romanization process occurred mostly through Catholic schools and religious movements, which appeal to urban, middle-class people.[4] Therefore, most poor people have been affected only marginally by the process.

Alberto Antoniazzi (1989) estimates that 80 to 85 percent of the Brazilian Catholic population is nonromanized.[5] But Catholicism is not a homogeneous phenomenon, and its degree of romanization varies, decreasing in rural areas among people who are poor and less educated. Therefore, if one considers only the poor population, there is virtually no romanization. The absence of the poor from the church became a concern among clergy and romanized laity in the 1960s, and the progressive Catholic church emerged from this concern. Eduardo Hoornaert (1988) stresses that progressive theologians have continued certain aspects of the romanization process. Their religious proposal has also rationalized religion and has tried to unify and embody lay people in the Catholic church. Despite being a product of the romanization process, the progressive church's plan is distinct from that of romanization. Instead of being concerned about the uniformity of religious dogma, beliefs, and moral behaviors, the progressive church attempts to unify political attitudes through the transformation of people's interpretation of the social world. Another major difference is the progressive church's concern with poor people. While the romanization proposal reached middle- and upper-class people, the progressive church is interested in reaching the poor.

THE CHRISTIAN BASE COMMUNITY (CEBS)

In its attempt to reach the lower sectors, the progressive church's most important instrument is the Christian Base Community (*Comunidade Eclesial de Base*, or CEB). These CEBs are small groups of poor lay Catholics who meet for prayer and meditation. They emerged in Latin America in the 1960s, spread rapidly, and became widely recognized in society by the 1970s. Most observers relate the emergence and growth of CEBs to the 1968 Conference of the Latin American Bishops (CELAM) held in Medellin, Colombia, but the Medellin conference only reinforced and acknowledged a phenomenon that had been developing since the early 1960s (Levine 1988).

There is no agreement as to the number of CEBs in Brazil. Jean Daudelin (1991) shows how early literature, which estimated 80,000 to 100,000 CEBs during the 1980s in Brazil, seems to have overestimated them by a factor of ten or more; actually, only a small minority of Catholics are engaged in these groups in Brazil.[6] Yet, despite their minority status,

CEBs have inspired a great deal of literature and debate among theologians, social scientists, the media, and the public because of their political intentions. Through CEBs, the progressive church proposes a radical democratization within the Catholic church and advocates such democratization for the broad society.

Because of their socialist political proposals and their support of the Sandinistas in the Nicaraguan Revolution (Dodson and Montgomery 1982; Lancaster 1987b), CEBs in Latin America acquired a reputation that was almost mythical. José Comblin (1987), a Belgian priest and writer who works in Brazil, describes the disappointment of foreigners who visited Brazilian CEBs, expecting them to demonstrate a higher degree of political awareness and engagement than they actually displayed.

The emergence of this mythical stature also resulted from the literature about CEB proposals and activities. The first studies about CEBs were written by theologians and religiously committed people who tended to emphasize descriptions of CEB projects, rather than the everyday reality of CEBs. One of the priests I interviewed said that this literature was intended to mobilize people to work in CEBs, rather than offer an actual assessment of this experience. Therefore, the literature avoided any analysis of the contradictions of everyday life in CEBs. Most of the authors had no practical experience in CEBs, according to Madeleine Adriance (1986) and Luíza Fernandes (1985).

Social scientists became interested in the CEB phenomenon in the 1980s, and scholars conducted studies on them. They analyzed the CEBs as instruments of political education and an application of the pedagogic method created by Paulo Freire, a Brazilian educator whose adult educational programs aimed at raising the social and political consciousness of the poor.[7] CEBs also attracted the attention of anthropologists, sociologists, and political scientists. Studies shifted from a discussion of the political projects of the progressive Catholic church to an analysis of CEB members' social characteristics, behavior, and attitudes.

CEBs do not emerge spontaneously among the poor, but are the fruits of pastoral agents' work. Pastoral agents can be seminarians, nuns, or lay people. Although some have poor origins and most live in the community in which they work, pastoral agents generally have moved from their home towns and have improved their level of education as a result of their work. Most, in fact, are college students or graduates. Poor people do not completely understand or accept the CEBs in the form proposed by these agents (Gómez de Souza 1989).

Although most authors agree that CEBs have emerged because of the work of "church intellectuals" and pastoral agents, few studies have been conducted about these groups. In fact, most studies have described only CEB members. The literature about CEBs has neglected pastoral agents, and some authors, such as Scott Mainwaring (1986), have tended to use the expression "base" or "grassroots" to refer to both pastoral agents and CEB members. Such language may obscure the differences between the groups. Analyses of the politicization of the Catholic church in Brazil also have neglected the importance of changes in the social origins of Brazilian clergy, who are now being recruited among lower social strata (Antoniazzi 1989).

There is no clear definition of CEBs (Bruneau 1982; Clearly 1985), which has caused problems for researchers. Theological definitions, such as that of Clodovis Boff, are not very useful for sociological analysis because they are abstract and do not reflect social reality. CEBs, in fact, can be socially very diverse. In my field research, I consider CEBs as Catholic groups of poor people that attempt, through meditation and prayer, to foster a view of religion that is socially and politically engaged. The groups I researched were Catholic progressive religious groups that aimed to increase people's participation not only in church activities and decisions but also in the society as a whole.

The most recent literature about CEBs is concerned with the crisis of the progressive church in Brazil and in Latin America.[8] The crisis of the church in Brazil can be explained not only by changes in the national political situation but also by the transformation of the church in Rome (Della Cava 1986). With Brazil's political opening of the 1980s (the so-called *Abertura*), some people left CEBs and joined new social movements and political parties that had emerged. On the international level, the Catholic church had become more conservative and was no longer supportive of the progressive sector. Pastoral agents interviewed in Rio de Janeiro and Recife noted that CEBs are no longer ranked among the first priorities of their dioceses, and Friar Betto, a well-known progressive Catholic intellectual, affirmed that the number of CEBs in Brazil fell dramatically in the late 1980s. As part of the international Catholic church's conservatism, conservative bishops have gained more power, while some progressive bishops have lost influence.[9] This shift, however, seems to have affected the hierarchy of priests, nuns, and pastoral agents more than ordinary CEB members. Another aspect of this shift is the Brazilian church's support of the Catholic Charismatic Movement, a Pentecostal version of Catholicism that has already spread widely, mainly among the middle class.

NONROMANIZED CATHOLICISM

The Gallup research about Brazilians' religious preferences mentioned earlier indicates that only 0.4 percent of Brazilians declare they follow Afro-Brazilian Spiritism (Carneiro and Soares 1992). All religious surveys in Brazil find a very low rate of people who declare that they practice Afro-Brazilian religion. Nevertheless, the number of Afro-Brazilian groups registered and the number of people who attend their celebrations, as well as other empirical elements, indicate that the actual figure must be much higher. In a survey questionnaire

where the interviewee has just one religious option with which
to identify, many Afro-Brazilian religious people will declare
themselves Catholic, not only because an Afro-Brazilian religious identity sometimes requires a kind of secrecy (Prandi
1991) or may face prejudice but also, and mainly, because they
do consider themselves Catholics. And they actually are Catholics, but a kind of nonromanized Catholics (Guimarães 1992).
As Dantas (1982, 1988) observes, in order to be initiated into a
Nagô cult (one kind of Afro-Brazilian religion), one has to be
baptized in the Catholic church. Thus, nonromanized Catholicism in Brazil comprises people with different religious practices, values, and beliefs. Some follow a traditional Catholicism
that is very similar to Portuguese Catholicism; others mix the
Portuguese elements with African and indigenous religious elements, resulting in a fusion of Catholic saints with African gods
and a mixture of various practices, rituals, and beliefs from each
of these traditions. There is a wide variety with different degrees of mixtures of Catholicism, Afro–Brazilian–Indian religions, and Kardecist Spiritism. In addition, Oriental religions
have recently become incorporated in this religious *bricolage*.
Despite their adoption of a religion that differs from the Roman
Catholic church, nonromanized Catholics, in general, consider
themselves Catholics and do not feel obliged to have an exclusive religious identity or affiliation. In Brazil it is common to
hear Catholic people say, "*Se fala de Deus, eu gosto*," meaning "I
like anyone who talks about God," leaving implicit the idea that
they are not tied to a single religion.[10]

The acceptance of new religious elements does not imply the
rejection of earlier ones. Catholicism has been able to unify the
diversity and has been flexible enough to embody a variety of
different traditions. This flexibility also exists among other religions, such as Buddhism and Hinduism, as Max Weber (1972)
observed. In fact, the exclusivity of religious identity is not
a common pattern among most religions but a peculiarity of
the Judeo-Protestant tradition, which is more rational in the

Weberian sense.[11] Nevertheless, romanized Catholicism of the twentieth century seems to follow the Protestant model.

Therefore, nonromanized Catholicism is a heterogeneous phenomenon that varies according to the predominance of one of the religious tendencies it has embodied. For instance, it can be predominantly composed of the rural Catholic tradition, or it can stress the elements of African-Brazilian, Brazilian indigenous, and other religious traditions. It is possible to identify three main tendencies within this broad concept of nonromanized Catholicism: rural Catholicism, Afro–Brazilian–Indian syncretism (here I refer to both as Brazilian popular or folk religion because they have their roots in poor sectors), and a middle-class and intellectualized tendency. The latter is composed of different syncretic currents involving religions that are also perceived as philosophies or "sciences," such as Oriental religions and Kardecist Spiritism (Aguiar 1978).

The oldest of these tendencies is rural Catholicism. The roots of this tradition are European, specifically Iberian. Similar beliefs and practices are shared by Portuguese, Spanish, and Latin American people (Tennekes 1985).[12] Rural Catholicism has the following characteristics: (1) a distant relationship to God and a focus on devotion to the saints and Mary, rather than Christ; (2) a direct and contractual relationship with the saints through *promessas*, the practice in which a person promises to offer something to a saint in return for being granted a specific request (e.g., some people promise to climb a hill on their knees if they are cured of an illness); (3) a general ignorance of the Gospels and the Bible; (4) the attribution of supernatural power to images and other religious objects; (5) privatization of the faith; and (6) the presence of lay leaders independent of the official Catholic church (Oliveira 1975). This distancing from the Roman church has allowed the development of messianic social movements around lay leaders;[13] of pilgrimages to shrines not accepted by the official church;[14] and the emergence of religious leaders, such as Father Cícero, a Brazilian priest excommunicated by the pope in 1920 but considered a saint by the people (Della Cava 1970).

Rural areas form the geographical basis of this tradition, and the official church's difficulties in reaching remote rural areas partly explain how this independent form of religiosity, which does not follow official models and doctrines, has remained strong for so long. Although rural Catholicism was clearly dominant in Brazil until the growth of Pentecostalism and the urban population explosion of the 1960s, its dominance has gradually declined, and its power has been shaken. Three main factors explain this change. First, the romanization process of the Brazilian church has fought traditional beliefs and practices it considered superstitions. Second, the migration of millions of Brazilians to large cities, which are the locus of Afro-Brazilian syncretist traditions, has blended traditional rural Catholicism with African beliefs. In addition, Pentecostalism appears to recruit most of its members from rural Catholicism.[15]

In contrast to rural Catholicism, the Afro–Brazilian–Indian tradition has become stronger with the modernization and urbanization of the country. In sharp contrast to all predictions by social scientists at the end of the nineteenth century and early in the twentieth century, such as R. Nina Rodrigues (1935), these religions have not disappeared but have bloomed and expanded with the growth of cities and industry.[16]

The existence of African cults in Brazil was reported in 1640 (Ribeiro 1982). The official Catholic church always fought these cults, a persecution perceived as the main cause of the so-called religious syncretism. Some authors, such as Juana Elbein dos Santos (1986), have argued that this persecution created a juxtaposition of African religion to Catholicism but did not generate an actual religious syncretism. They affirm that persecution made people hide their religious affiliation to African religion and declare themselves Catholic in order to avoid further persecution and prejudice. For these authors, syncretism is a myth; people do not actually "syncretize" or identify the two religions. This idea is also defended by leaders of the black movement.

The trend within Afro-Brazilian religions that searches for the African purity of their traditions emerged under the influence of the first anthropologists in the region in the 1930s, who protected the more traditional groups against political repression (Dantas 1982). But the majority of Afro-Brazilian Spiritists do not question this mixture and believe there is no contradiction in the syncretism. These people believe in Catholic saints as well as African gods, the *orixás* (Medeiros 1988; Motta 1983).

The government persecuted Afro-Brazilian Spiritists until 1945 (Brown 1986; Prandi 1991), and Afro-Brazilian Spiritist groups are still required to register with local police departments. The elimination of these cults and of syncretism also has been an objective of romanization in Brazil. Examples of such attempts are the books of Fr. Boaventura Kloppenburgo, O.F.M. (1960). The Catholic hierarchy tried at that time to "purify" Catholicism from superstitions. It did not succeed.

At present, when the progressive Catholic church is trying to accept the African presence in Catholicism (Medeiros 1991),[17] leaders of black movements are trying to reverse this fusion, which they consider a cultural domination of blacks by whites. But despite the efforts of both the romanized church in the 1940s and 1950s and the black movement in the 1980s, people insist on keeping their multiple religious identity as Catholic and Afro-Brazilian Spiritist. This explains why the census and other research have consistently found a very small percentage of people who identify themselves as Afro-Brazilian Spiritists.

Although some African and Brazilian Indian elements can be found in rural areas, the development of Afro–Brazilian–Indian syncretic cults has occurred mainly in the major cities, especially Rio de Janeiro, Salvador, Recife, and São Luis, all of which have large black populations. The diversity within this tradition has reflected the various African backgrounds and the presence or predominance of Brazilian Indian elements. One of the many existing classifications of these various traditions is that presented by Roberto Motta (1992) who conducted his research in Recife, in northeastern Brazil. Motta describes three major categories: (1) African tradition only (Nagô and Gêge), named Candomblé-Xangô;[18] (2) a mix of Brazilian Indian and African traditions with a predominance of African tradition (Catimbó-Jurema); and (3) Umbanda.

Umbanda is the most popular and recent fusion of Afro–Brazilian–Indian Catholic tradition with French Kardecist Spiritism (Birman 1983; Brown 1986). This syncretism offers a theoretical explanation that is able to integrate different Catholic and African beliefs and rituals. In addition to the creation of a global theoretical system of interpretation, Umbanda also proposes a moral ethic and universal values. Therefore, despite its magical and ritualistic elements, Umbanda may be seen as a partial process of rationalization, in the Weberian sense, of more traditional Afro-Brazilian and indigenous syncretic tendencies, generically called Candomblé.[19] Roberto Motta (1992) has written about the existence of the "umbandization" process and classifies these religious cults in a continuum that ranges from *less* "umbandizated" to *more* "umbandizated."

Despite its origins in the poorest stratum of society, the descendants of slaves, the Afro-Brazilian religion, both Candomblé and Umbanda, has now reached all social levels (Prandi 1991). As Diana Brown (1986) demonstrates, Umbanda performs an important role in the process of upward mobility of these religious traditions. Proponents of Umbanda have sought to make Afro-Spiritism more acceptable by denying its black origins and by stressing charity.

There is a third syncretic tendency, which is characteristic of middle-class sectors and less popular among poor people. The most important middle-class fusion is that of Catholicism with the pure Kardecist Spiritism brought to the country at the end of the nineteenth century by Brazilians who studied in France (Brown 1986). Another middle-class and more recent syncretism is that of Catholicism with Buddhism and other Oriental religions. Despite the fact that some of these groups offer alternative religious identities to Catholicism, many people who join these groups keep their Catholic identities (Cabral da Silva 1988).

The first and second kinds of syncretisms are those more popular among the poor: rural Catholicism and Afro-Brazilian Spiritism. Despite some divergence on moral patterns and beliefs between the two tendencies, there are important common features between them, which allow me to consider them together. This commonality is particularly important when compared with Protestantism and the Catholicism of CEBs.

PROTESTANTISM

In Brazil, only Protestants reject embodiment and identification with the Catholic church (Antoniazzi 1989). Protestantism requires an exclusive religious affiliation. Therefore, it not only rejects Catholicism but also confronts the whole idea of religious syncretism and nonexclusive religious identity of the non-romanized Catholicism and other religious traditions in Brazil.

Protestantism first arrived in Brazil in the nineteenth century, and the first Protestant churches were immigrant and missionary churches (Leonard 1963). Immigrant churches were founded in Brazil only to continue the tradition of their immigrant members, not to engage in active recruiting measures. This is true of the Lutheran church in southern Brazil. In contrast, the missionary churches, such as the Methodist and the Baptist, came to Brazil in order to recruit new followers.

Although the first Protestant missionaries arrived in Brazil in 1810, the growth of Protestantism became significant only after the Pentecostal renewal.[20] Before the spread of Pentecostalism, only the Baptist church was able to gain members among low-income people. The other churches had very few converts; most of them were middle-class people.[21] On the contrary, Pentecostal Protestantism was able to reach the poor in Brazil. As a result of the importance of Pentecostalism, the dichotomy involving the Protestantism of immigration versus the Protestantism of missions lost its importance. The distinction between Pentecostal and historical Protestantism became more crucial to understanding these churches.

Three Pentecostal churches were matrices for all other Brazilian Pentecostal churches: *Assembléia de Deus* (the Assembly of God), *Congregação Cristã do Brasil* (the Christian Congregation of Brazil) and *Igreja do Evangelho Quadrangular* (the Foursquare Gospel Church) (Rolim 1985). The first Pentecostal church in Brazil, the Assembly of God, was founded by Swedish missionaries in 1911. These missionaries were Baptists who discovered the Pentecostal renewal in the United States and went to a Brazilian Baptist church in the northern state of Para to evangelize. They led a group of dissidents in this Baptist church, which became the Assembly of God. The second-oldest Pentecostal church in Brazil, the Christian Congregation of Brazil, was founded by an Italian missionary who also became a Pentecostal in the United States and later came to Brazil. The Foursquare Gospel has a direct American origin. The first missionary from this church traveled to Brazil from the United States in the 1950s.

All three churches grew, suffered internal conflicts, and split, creating other denominations. The Brazil for Christ Church (*Igreja Brasil para Cristo*) was founded by a former member of the Assembly of God who later joined the Foursquare Gospel and then decided to found his own church (Rolim 1985). The Assembly of God also gave birth to the church *Deus é Amor* (God is Love) and the *Igreja Pentecostal Assembléia de Deus* (the Pentecostal Assembly of God Church), among others.

At present, a great variety of Pentecostal churches exists in Brazil. In addition to the "neo-Pentecostalism" phenomenon, that is, the "pentecostalization" or Pentecostal renewal in the historical Protestant churches, a new kind of Pentecostal church that is more concerned with healing has emerged and developed during the past ten years. These churches have been identified in the sociological literature as peripheral Pentecostalism, or *Movimento de Cura Divina* (Movement for Divine Healing) (Mendonça and Velasques 1990). Examples of this type of church include *Casa da Benção* (House of Blessing), and the growing, *Igreja Universal do Reino de Deus* (Universal Church of the Reign of God) and *Igreja Internacional da Graça Divina* (International Church of the Divine Grace).[22] Most of these churches, such as the Universal Church of the Reign of God (better known as *Igreja Universal*), have less restrictive moral regulations than traditional Pentecostal churches do (Rubim 1990). They are more concerned with expelling the Afro-Brazilian spirits identified as evil spirits and healings. Exorcism services on Friday evenings are very popular. The Universal Church of the Reign of God is also growing outside Brazil.[23]

As mentioned earlier, Pentecostalism is also now a phenomenon within the historical Protestant churches. Many historical denominations face conflicts because of this phenomenon. There are now the *Igreja Batista Renovada* (Renewed Baptist Church) and the *Igreja Presbiteriana Renovada* (Renewed Presbyterian Church), which are the fruits of a split within the Baptist and Presbyterian churches brought on by Pentecostalism. People from the *Renovadas* are mostly from the middle class and socially more similar to those who belong to the Catholic Charismatic Movement than to Pentecostals from the traditional Pentecostal churches and from the new churches, such as the *Igreja Universal do Reino de Deus*. The data in this book refer to traditional Pentecostalism, which is still the denomination that attracts more of the Brazilian poor. Almost all my Pentecostal interviewees are from the Assembly of God, the largest Protestant denomination in Brazil.

Despite its phenomenal growth, Protestants in Brazil are still only 8.5 percent of the entire population, according to a Gallup survey (Carneiro and Soares 1992). In the 1980 Brazilian census, Protestants represented 7 percent of the Brazilian population, and Pentecostals accounted for more than half of the Protestant population. This proportion is higher among low-income people. There are no data for the whole society that link income to religious affiliation. Some local research in poor areas does indicate a more significant presence of Pentecostalism in these areas than in Brazil as a whole. Macedo (1986), for instance, shows that 17 percent of the population of a poor neighborhood in São Paulo is Protestant.

In the neighborhood of Alto José do Pinho in Recife, I observed five Protestant but only two Catholic churches, and I noticed there a higher attendance at Sunday Protestant services than at the Catholic Masses and celebrations. These observations are reinforced by declarations from neighborhood residents.

The popularity of Pentecostalism among the Brazilian poor has attracted the attention of social scientists. The first question they raise deals with the relationship between Pentecostalism and social change. Some authors interpret the growth of Pentecostalism not only as an indicator of social change but also as a factor in modernization and improvement for the poor (Roberts 1968; Willems 1967). Other authors do not view Pentecostalism as fostering social change. On the contrary, they stress the political conservatism of the Pentecostal message and perceive this movement as not only fostering political withdrawal, but also hindering social change.[24] Because of the political conservatism of the Pentecostal worldview, many authors have conducted research on Pentecostal political behavior, but there are controversies about this issue. Unlike the authors above, Regina Novaes (1985), Sandra Stoll (1986), and Hans Tennekes (1985) observe that Pentecostal political behavior is not always conservative.[25] It seems to depend on circumstances.

These authors suggest that the Pentecostal political attitude is more affected by the political situation in the country, or local political alliances, than by religious values. Other authors stress the political importance of the congregational organization of Pentecostal churches for the poor. This kind of organization allows the development of poor people's leadership and ideological autonomy because the poor can head their own religious institutions (Brandão 1980).

Another question that intrigues researchers is how such an ascetic and restrictive morality is acceptable to people with such a multiple, flexible, and syncretic worldview as the Brazilian folk culture possesses (Aubrée 1984). This question leads to another one: Who becomes a Pentecostal? Research shows that Pentecostalism initially grew mostly among the poor of large cities who had recently migrated from rural areas (Broody 1973; César 1973; Fry and Howe 1975). Francisco Rolim (1980) observes that Pentecostals worked predominantly in commerce and service sectors. The growth of Pentecostalism was at first related to the anomie of the great metropolitan areas; however, Pentecostalism soon became popular among the poor in rural areas (Hoffnagel 1978; Novaes 1985). Data collected in Managua (Lancaster 1987a) and Rio de Janeiro (Broody 1973) suggest that most Pentecostals are drawn from the lowest stratum among the poor. Therefore, researchers began to relate Pentecostalism to poverty rather than anomie. Yet, despite being composed mainly of the poorest stratum, the Pentecostal Protestant churches in Brazil have experienced a great growth and enrichment as institutions.[26] They are not only numerous but have also attained economic power and influence. Pentecostal leaders now control television stations in Brazil, as well as publishing houses and radio stations.[27] There is little available data about the financial organization of Pentecostal churches. They receive economic help from Protestant churches overseas, but they also generate their own resources from members' contributions. These churches also have obtained political power by electing several church members as political representatives (Freston 1988). A question that has interested many researchers, and one that I address here, is whether such improvement occurs among poor Pentecostal church members as well. Would Protestant Pentecostalism be more useful for the economic improvement of the Brazilian poor than other religions?

CHAPTER II

Coping with Poverty
and Religious Affiliation
in Brazil

Hélio Jaguaribe et al. (1986) affirm that more than half the Brazilian population is poor, but how we measure poverty is very controversial. The method most often used is an income test, those falling under a certain income being defined as poor. The controversy surrounding this method is over where the poverty line should be drawn.[1] For instance, Jorge Jatobá (1988) considers as poor those whose families earn less than one-fourth of the minimum wage per capita: namely, those people who do not earn enough to survive physically. In contrast, Jaguaribe et al. (1986) define the poor not only as those who are unable to obtain the goods necessary for their material survival but also as those who must spend their entire income to obtain these goods—the poverty line thus equaling the personal income of two minimum wages. Jatobá's earlier test referred to a situation of misery, rather than poverty. Not only have many economic studies shown the low buying power of the Brazilian minimum wage, this fact is also acknowledged by government policies. For example, the housing program for poor people in Brazil subsidizes housing only for those whose family income is higher than three minimum wages (Moura 1988). Although families whose income per capita is equal to two minimum wages are relatively less poor than those whose income equals one minimum wage, in absolute terms of the quality of life they are nevertheless poor.

Absolute poverty in Brazil is a result of social class. In contrast to what occurs in developed countries (Sidel 1986), the people who live in absolute poverty in Brazil are composed of more than the elderly, the unemployed, the sick, or the most unskilled workers. In Brazil, not only those who are out of the job market and cannot work are deprived of basic goods, but also some of "those who labor the hardest."[2] Almost 25 percent of the people whose family income was less than one-fourth of one minimum wage per capita were employed in the formal sector (Jatobá 1988). Yet another element that demonstrates the class nature of Brazilian poverty is the fact that the poverty is persistent. The Brazilian poor normally spend all their lives in poverty. For most, poverty is not a temporary situation—an economic crisis that lasts only a few difficult years, as is the case for most of the poor in the United States (Sidel 1986). But the correlation between poverty and social class does not mean that there is a homogeneity among the poor. On the contrary, as many authors have demonstrated, the Brazilian poor are very diverse and differ in relation to their degree of poverty (Niemayer 1979; Zaluar 1985). According to Jaguaribe et al. (1986), those considered poor vary in their plight from living in misery to living in strict poverty. Those who earn more than one minimum wage but no more than two are considered to be living in "strict poverty"—they are not able to supply their basic needs other than the merest physical subsistence—and in 1985 this group comprised 25 percent of the employed and self-employed Brazilian population. Below this level is an intermediate level of poor people who earn from one-half to one minimum wage. These people are viewed as "indigents" and were estimated to comprise 22.8 percent of the employed and self-employed Brazilian population in 1985. The lowest level of the poor are those who earn less than one-half a minimum wage. They are estimated to be 13.4 percent of the population and are considered to be living in a condition of misery (Jaguaribe et al. 1986).

The poor people of Brazil are not concentrated only in rural areas (Valle Silva 1991), but there is a regional difference, with more poor people living in the Brazilian Northeast than in any other region. Brazil is a country of contrasting regional inequalities.[3] In addition, according to Jaguaribe and others, the percentage of poor women is higher than that of poor men.[4] The quality of life within these different categories of poverty is also slightly different. Therefore, within the limits of a poor neighborhood, an internal social stratification develops. The less poor within a particular area—those who are the better-off among the poor—become the elite of that area.

But overall there is limited opportunity for social mobility and improvement of life conditions. To move from one stratum to another within the different levels of poverty is more common than to leave the low-income stratum and overcome poverty.[5] Mobility therefore tends to be circular and within a stratum and, within the low-income sector, is very much based on an individual's personal characteristics. The fact that the better-off among the poor are not able to provide their families with goods other than those necessary for their physical survival limits their children's ability to overcome their poverty. The subjective experience of being poor differs depending on the individual's position in each of the different levels. But even those people who are the best-off among the poor clearly face obstacles in rising out of poverty and almost unsurmountable class barriers. Almost nothing isolated individuals can do allows their upward mobility to another stratum of society. In contrast, the situation of the poorest of the poor may very well depend on their personal characteristics. For those who recover from a health problem, obtain a new job, or learn new skills, there can be a certain improvement in the quality of life.

Therefore, the stratification within the low-income sectors depends additionally on these individuals' abilities to cope with poverty. Those who better endure poverty may become the elite among the poor. Depending on the social and economic context, their political orientation, and the social organizations they belong to, these individuals may strive for social transformation or may leave this sector.

Thus, despite limited opportunities for financial improvement among the poor in Brazil, some families are more successful in solving their economic problems than others. Some people are even able to overcome poverty or, at least, to offer their children a chance to become upwardly mobile. The question is whether religion has any influence on this process.

THE SOCIOECONOMIC SITUATION
OF PENTECOSTALS

Some researchers have hypothesized, based on Weber's theory of the economic advantage of the Protestant ethic in a capitalist society, that after conversion to Protestantism, people in Latin America generally improve their economic condition.[6] We also find that Pentecostal pastors and church members share this belief (Flora 1976; Hoffnagel 1978; Novaes 1985; Coral-Prieto 1980). Pentecostal Protestants also claim to experience economic improvement after their conversion. One Pentecostal pastor from the Assembly of God in São Paulo, for example, stressed the positive economic consequences for the poor who convert to the Assembly of God. As evidence, he testified that

Assembly of God churches located in the *favelas* (slums) tend to lose their membership because of the relocation of their members to "better" areas as their lives improved economically. Nevertheless, thus far there is no research that verifies this hypothesis. On the contrary, different authors who examined the same question, among them Claude Lalive D'Epinay (1969), Cordelia Flora (1976), Judith Hoffnagel (1978), and Bryan Roberts (1968), concluded that, in fact, Pentecostals in Latin America did not experience more upward mobility than people with other religious affiliations. Notwithstanding the growth and enrichment of Pentecostal churches and some of their pastors, the material conditions of life of most Pentecostal people did not change substantially. Most, however, testified to an improvement in other aspects of their lives, such as spiritual peace, better health, and a more stable personal and familial economy as a consequence of overcoming health problems.

Judith Hoffnagel (1978, 43) suggests that the Assembly of God church in Recife, the coastal northeastern city of about 1.3 million inhabitants where I did part of my field research, does not recruit "its membership from the very bottom of the Brazilian class structure." She finds an illiteracy rate of 19 percent among the members of this church, which is lower than the regional illiteracy rate, which in 1980 was 47 percent (Jaguaribe et al. 1986). Based on Assembly of God members' illiteracy rate and occupations, Hoffnagel (1978, 49) concludes that they are not the poorest in the society. Nevertheless, in later research in Recife, a higher illiteracy rate was seen among Pentecostals from different churches, suggesting that the trend is for more of the very poor to be attracted to Pentecostalism (Aubrée 1984, 139). These more recent data agree with Roger N. Lancaster's (1987b, 183–84) research in Nicaragua, suggesting that traditional Pentecostal churches recruit most of their members among the lowest stratum of the poor, many of whom are alcoholics or sick or elderly people. Accordingly, the economic situation of Pentecostals immediately before their conversion tends to be the most precarious and unstable among the poor. Those who become Pentecostals also tend to have more personal problems than those who engage in the CEBs, Pentecostalism being more attractive than the CEBs for these people because it offers more immediate solutions to their problems.

An analysis of the 1980 census of the state of Pernambuco in Brazil indicates that there are more Pentecostal women than men in Pernambuco. It also shows that older people account for a greater portion of church membership than do young people. There is an overrepresentation of people aged fifty and older. The less represented tend to be between twenty and twenty-nine years old (Silva 1987). Because women and older people earn less and have fewer opportunities to improve their lives than men and the young do, and because some of these people convert at an age when there are few chances for improving their lives, they tend to face more economic problems, and so it is difficult to estimate the economic consequences of their religion.

Despite the fact that a reasonable number of young people convert to Pentecostalism (Burdick 1990), the young do not remain long in the traditional Pentecostal churches. Celeste, the daughter of the founder of the Assembly of God church in the Alto José do Pinho neighborhood in Recife, refused to participate in her father's church when she was young. She also noted that none of her brothers followed her father's faith. Another interviewee, Raquel, mentioned that it is typical for young men to stay away from the church. Most of the children of the Pentecostals, in fact, leave their parents' church during their teen years, some returning to these churches after they marry.

The relative absence of young men from the Pentecostal churches is clearly noticeable in the Sunday school of the Assembly of God of Alto José do Pinho in Recife. Here, people are separated by age and largely by sex into six groups: two for children of both sexes, one for young women, two for *senhoras* (i.e., married or older women), and one for men.

Anésio is typical of a man who converts to Pentecostalism when faced with no other means to improve his life. Anésio came to Recife looking for a job and found one in a factory. Later, when he became ill from the chemicals used at the factory, the church helped him spiritually. "The factory disabled me, and I found comfort in God," he says. Having retired for reasons of health in 1965, he has been a believer ever since. Before his conversion, he frequently danced, gambled, drank, and smoked; but after conversion, his life was different. "With the Gospel I changed," he says. "Nowadays my inclination is only for Jesus' work. I am retired, my income is low, but God multiplies it. My money is enough now."

Faced with problems and material difficulties, Neusa exemplifies another instance of conversion, although Neusa's is the sole case of a person alleging more problems after conversion. Neusa never mentioned any economic improvement in her family life. "My life in the Gospel is a life of suffering," she said. Neusa's major problem was her alcoholic husband. She recounted that even before conversion, she was always dedicated to work, but her husband's drinking caused her much suffering. After her conversion, her problems with her husband increased because he opposed her participation in the church, preferring Afro-Spiritism. Some years later, however, her husband, who had retired because of health problems, not only stopped drinking but also converted to Pentecostalism. This was the period during which they had a somewhat greater economic stability. They had little money, Neusa said, but it was enough ("*era pouco, mas dava*") because her husband had become more responsible. But soon afterward, Neusa's husband died. Neusa believes that God wanted to test her again. For her, God's blessing does not necessarily imply happiness and material comfort. As a widow, she needs to work as a housekeeper in order to raise her eight small children. The case of Neusa also illustrates the limitations of a single woman with children to improve their economic condition.

Creuza referred to her economic improvement after her conversion as God's blessing. She explained how she worked hard
and had her own business in a small town in northeastern Brazil. Then, in search of a better life, she migrated with her husband and children to Rio de Janeiro. There her husband went
a long time before finding a job, and in the interim he became
an alcoholic. Finally, when Creuza became ill and could not
work, they had no food for their five children. In order to eat,
she had to beg. Humiliated and desperate, she made *promes-*
sas to Catholic saints and followed the advice of Afro-Brazilian
Spiritists to find a job for her husband. Nothing worked, so she
decided to make a vow, or *promessa*, to the God of the *crentes*
(believers), the name by which the Pentecostals are known: "O
God of the Believers, give my husband a job. Do not allow me
to beg anymore and allow me to have enough to eat. If you
give my husband a job, I will be a believer. I will not have my
hair cut anymore, I will not wear makeup anymore, and I will
dress only with long sleeves." The next day, a relative offered
her husband a job. Creuza kept her vow. Soon she recovered her
health, and through working and saving their lives improved.
She interprets her achievements as God's blessing for both her
hard work and her ascetic behavior. As a member of the church,
she not only learned to read so that she could read the Bible
but she also became a religious leader. Some years later, her
husband also converted. At present, she is satisfied with her economic position, which is among the upper strata of their *favela*.
Although Creuza's ascetic Pentecostal behavior has been very
instrumental in her economic success, it seems that Pentecostalism merely gave meaning and support to her previous abilities
and that she became a Pentecostal because she believed that her
promessa to God was responsible for her husband's obtaining a
job. Pentecostalism may have helped her overcome a crisis, but
only indirectly did it help her attain her later achievements.

There are also conversions among those who are not in crisis,
though these seem to be fewer. In contrast to Anésio, Creuza,

and Neusa, Maria José was not facing economic difficulties when she converted. Like Anésio, Maria José stresses the spiritual, rather than material, gains of her conversion. Her life history describes her struggle to survive, the difficult period of her husband's unemployment, and her efforts to find a job and pursue her own career. But it was only after becoming a widow that she became a Pentecostal. Although the death of her husband did not result in an economic crisis, she explains that she felt a spiritual dissatisfaction when he died. "My soul cried out for something else," she says. "Sometimes it happens that a person has bread, clothing, but is not happy. I was missing something . . . my soul was not happy." As with Anésio, Pentecostalism did not help Maria José's life to improve economically. Instead, it helped her to keep what she had already attained and helped her to be happy.

The case of Edson differs from that of Maria José because he converted when he was relatively young. Although only twenty years old at the time of his conversion, Edson was already an alcoholic. For him to join the Assembly of God, he had to stop drinking, which helped him obtain a regular job. Therefore, conversion clearly changed his life and economic conditions. When interviewed, Edson was trying to convert his alcoholic brother. In Edson's case, Pentecostalism helped him endure poverty better by giving him more opportunities to improve. As with the husbands of Neusa and Creuza, Edson experienced an immediate improvement in his life when he stopped drinking. Others say they are amazed at how much better Edson looks since having become a believer.

Sebastião and Zeferino, from a rural part of the state of Pernambuco, had converted and moved to Recife, the capital, for a better life when they were still young. Despite the ascetic behavior they had practiced during their whole lives, they did not improve their economic situations. Now, as old men, both are still poor, and most of their children did not improve any more than they had.

Some of those interviewed in Recife, like Baruc and Levi, were raised Pentecostals by their parents, who themselves had been Pentecostals for most of their lives. But their lives, like their parents, remained poor, never showing any significant improvement. The parents and children did reach a high enough stratum among the poor for each to be able to buy his own home. Baruc, for example, was even able to finish college,[7] but he is still unemployed; he has not escaped the family's lifelong poverty. Perhaps, as David Martin (1990) sees it, such people have a latent possibility for upward mobility that a broad improvement in the Brazilian economy might allow to surface.

There are also examples of young people who leave the church when they reach better economic and social situations. A case in point is that of Licia, an ex-factory worker from Rio de Janeiro who once lived in a *favela*. Despite the Protestant background of her family, she became a member of the Assembly of God only on recovering from a health and psychological crisis at the age of twenty. After becoming a young leader in her church, she decided to study college-level theology. Through her studies and her contacts with people from other Protestant denominations and other socioeconomic levels, she began to question her previous beliefs and found herself in conflict with her church. At the time of my interview with her, her life had improved to the extent that she was no longer working in a factory; she had a bureaucratic job at City Hall and was also studying law. She had left the Assembly of God for the more liberal Presbyterian church. As Maria da Graça Floriano and Regina Novaes (1985) have reported about the Baptist church in Brazil, young men who become pastors have more of a chance to improve their lives than those who do not become pastors. It has also been shown that economic improvement occurs among Afro-Brazilian Spiritist leaders.

Despite examples of economic betterment, for the poor people of Brazil there are few opportunities for economic improvement and little upward mobility. The lack of opportunity is even greater for families whose heads of households are sick, alcoholic, elderly, or single female. When people's lives do improve, such as in Creuza's family, the potential for upward mobility is limited, most often restricted to within the class from which they came. Some Pentecostals, however, are not able to improve their situation even within the limits of their class. Most frequently, however, they do succeed in coping with poverty well enough to survive and not move farther down the economic ladder. Still, very few ever attain a middle-class standard of life or can provide their children with the opportunity to attain it; even with a college degree, the chances of earning sufficient money to enjoy a middle-class standard of living are very unlikely for children born of poverty. There is, however, intraclass mobility; that is, those who finish their studies generally become the elite of their class.

Examples of illiterates whose children obtained a college degree can be found both among illiterate Pentecostals and illiterates of other religions. Zezé and Baruc, for example, are children of illiterate Pentecostals who have earned college degrees. The same phenomenon among non-Pentecostals can be seen in Zezé's cousins, who were not raised Pentecostal but who also graduated from college. According to Zezé, some of these cousins attained even better economic positions than hers. Wilson, for example, whose parents were not particularly religious, obtained a university degree in history and was teaching in a high school. Similar examples were found among Spiritists: The daughter of the Spiritist Maria not only attained a good education but also a well-paying job. Despite being illiterate, Pinça, a "mother of saint" (that is, a religious leader) in Umbanda, has a son who studied law. The Umbandista Conceição has a son who succeeded in passing the *vestibular* (a difficult and highly competitive examination one must take in order to obtain a place at the university), but he studied only briefly at the university.

Regardless of their religious options, most of Brazil's poor are motivated to improve their condition, to study, and to adopt behaviors that will prove functional in an industrial society, such as disciplined work habits and some accumulation of savings. Brazilian society seems to be industrial and modern enough to offer a "secular plausibility structure" that affirms these values. Nevertheless, in situations where lack of work or poor health offer little chance to improve oneself, Pentecostals are more motivated than others to survive by avoiding self-destructive behavior, such as drinking and gambling. The secular worldview tends to consider those who face such crises as helpless failures; in this respect, Pentecostal opposition to the secular worldview is very important. Pentecostalism helps people to believe that they can overcome their difficulties. Because of this, Pentecostalism seems to be more useful for those in crisis than for those "on their feet." As Bryan Roberts (1968) suggests, Pentecostals seem to endure poverty better than people of other religious groups. This does not necessarily mean that they are better prepared to overcome their poverty.

THE SOCIOECONOMIC SITUATION OF CEB MEMBERS

It is more difficult to draw a social profile of CEB members than of Pentecostals because of the limited amount of quantifiable data on them and because of the diversity of the CEB experience. As Bruneau (1982) observes, quite different groups may all be defined as CEBs. In addition, CEBs of different geographical areas seem to attract different kinds of people. Rural CEBs, urban CEBs, CEBs in areas of open and strong social conflict, and CEBs living amid less social conflict seem to recruit members with distinctly different characteristics.

The lack of a clear definition has created operational problems for CEB research in the archdiocese of Olinda and Recife in northeastern Brazil. In 1984, when Gustavo Castro did field research in the archdiocese, the term CEB was rarely used there, although it became more common after 1985. Nevertheless, this archdiocese was considered a pioneer in CEB experiments because of the grassroots evangelization movement created by Dom Helder Câmara in 1969: *Movimento de Evangelização Encontro de Irmãos*, or Movement of Evangelization Meeting with Siblings (Gregory 1971).

This evangelization movement has attempted to create among the poor small groups who gather for prayer, reflection, and social activities. The agendas and goals of these groups are the same as those of CEBs; however, they differ from CEBs in that they do not serve as substitutes for the parish structure. Instead, they have much the same type of organization as middle-class religious movements. The grassroots evangelization groups of *Movimento de Evangelhização Encontro de Irmãos* are independent of their local priests and are linked directly to the archdiocese. But the archdiocese chooses local priests who are especially dedicated to the movement. Local clergy and lay leaders consider CEBs to be a recent phenomenon in the city of Recife and the state of Pernambuco. Gustavo Castro (1987), however, tried to show that the *Movimento Encontro de Irmãos* displayed the most important characteristics of CEBs. Therefore, it is somewhat misleading to differentiate CEBs from groups created by the grassroots evangelization movement. Even so, the hierarchy in this archdiocese prefers not to call these groups CEBs. The CEBs I researched in Pernambuco were composed primarily of former members of the *Movimento de Evangelhização Encontro de Irmãos*. Sometimes these people still identify themselves as members of the movement. Actually, the expression CEB is not used by the Catholic poor in Recife. It is not common among poor people in the state of Rio de Janeiro either. In both areas, only the word *community* is used.

The only national data available on the CEBs are those collected through registration forms from their national meetings, such as the Seventh Interecclesiastic Meeting of CEBs, which

was held in Caxias, state of Rio de Janeiro, in 1989 (Centro
Ecumênico de Documentação e Informação CEDI, 1989) and
the Sixth Interecclesiastic Meeting of CEBs, which was held
in Trindade, in the state of Goias, in 1986 (Arquidiocese de
Goiânia 1986, 688–89). These data refer only to the CEB leadership, however, and may not describe the ordinary CEB member. Therefore such data cannot be the basis for any generalizations about CEBs. In both the 1989 and 1986 meetings, for
instance, there was a larger percentage of men in attendance
than women. In 1986, about 61 percent of the participants were
men; in 1989, men constituted 55 percent. By contrast, more
women were in attendence at local CEB meetings and meetings among the local leadership. For instance, in two observed
meetings among the local leadership of CEBs in the metropolitan area of Recife, there were many more women than men. At
one such meeting, 74 percent of the participants were women;
at another, there were two men, ten children, and thirty-three
women, including one nun. At another meeting, in Caxias, Rio
de Janeiro, there were twenty women and twelve men, not including three priests and seven nuns. Several researchers have
also noted an overall higher proportion of female membership
to male membership in the CEBs (see Castro 1987; Levine
1988; Petrini 1984).

Although I am aware of the difficulty with generalizations,
in order to obtain some data on the social characteristics of
CEB people in an area outside Recife, called Igarassu, in the
state of Pernambuco, I distributed fifty questionnaires at a local
meeting of representatives from sixteen CEBs.

The data show that more women (74 percent) attended the
meeting than men and that more people were without jobs
than with jobs. Only 36 percent in the study were economically active; of these, 12 percent worked on their own and 24
percent were otherwise employed. Most of those involved in
no paid activity were housewives (24 percent), while the unemployed amounted to 20 percent and retired people formed

another 6 percent.[8] Again, these data differ from data collected at the national meetings mentioned earlier. In Caxias, for instance, only 8.4 percent were unemployed and 9 percent were retired; there was a much higher participation of employed people (43.1 percent) (CEDI 1989).

The years of schooling for participants at the Igarassu meeting were higher than average among the poor, more than half the participants claiming at least some years at the *Ginásio* level or higher, meaning that they had five or more years of schooling.[9] People at local leadership meetings also had a better economic background and situation than the majority of ordinary Pentecostals interviewed. But their economic situation seemed not to have been affected by their affiliation with the CEBs. CEB members never reported any job or health improvements after joining a CEB. In contrast to findings among Pentecostals, no CEB member interviewed had formerly been an alcoholic, and only one woman reported having an alcoholic husband.

In São Paulo, Ted Hewitt (1988) observed the absence of the neediest poor among the CEBs. This was also noted by some of the CEB leadership interviewed, such as Odete from Alto José do Pinho, Recife. Odete said that no one in her group needed the food distributed by the group in order to survive.

Despite facing economic difficulties and being aware of their relative poverty and less-than-privileged position in society, CEB members know that they are better off than most people in their neighborhood, and sometimes even refer to neighbors as "the others." Alice, a CEB leader from Alto do Carneiro, Recife, explained how her meditation group came to the realization that it must not *fazer para o povo, mas fazer com o povo* ("must not do *for* the poor but *with* them"). (Note that the Portuguese word *povo* can be literally translated into English as "people," but actually it carries the connotation "poor people.") As Alice's statement implies, her meditation group did not see itself as *povo*; the *povo* were "the others." Another instance of this phenomenon came from an interviewee named Ernestina, who in comparing the street where she lived with other streets in the neighborhood, explained the need to help the poor.

The CEB leaders interviewed were aware that the poorest of the poor could not participate in CEBs. Margarida, from Rio de Janeiro, told of a man her group helped when he was sick, explaining that he could not belong to the group because being so poor and having so many children, he would not have the time. In general, CEB activities are not aimed at helping people with their personal problems. On the contrary, CEBs often require members to dedicate part of the time available to them for personal and family needs to the community. Therefore, personal problems would tend to keep people from participating in CEBs, rather than draw them to these groups, as is the case with Pentecostal churches. Margarida, for example, explained that when serious health problems occurred in her family, these problems kept her from participating in CEBs.

The most probable explanation for the low male participation in these groups is the lack of time. Aninha, for instance, said that her husband approved of her activities at CEBs, but because of his job, he did not have the time to join her and participate in the religious movement. Another woman, named Ilze, explained that she stopped going to CEB meetings after she got a job. Most CEB leaders and members were women without jobs outside the home, who could allocate their time as they wished. Most men in the CEBs I visited also did not have jobs. Lúcio, for example, had been unemployed; when he found a job, he stopped attending CEB meetings. Aniceto is able to attend because he is retired. Margarida confirmed that in her CEB most of the men are unemployed; they end up doing jobs wherever and whenever they find them—known in Brazil as *fazer biscate* (to do odd jobs). Thus the demands of a job seem to be incompatible with the demands of CEBs. Margarida explained, for instance, that the sole factory worker in her CEB left the group because he was afraid that participation in it would threaten his job; in his case, he did not agree with some of the political ideas of the group. He thought that by engaging in the CEB's political protests he would lose his job, stressing the shortage of jobs and his need to be employed in order to support his family. Here we see that the conflict between engaging in CEB activities and the job market seems to have two dimensions: both CEBs and the job are time-consuming, and CEBs require an ideological attitude that may conflict with that required by the job market.

The problem of time is the most often given explanation for the weak appeal of CEBs among the working poor, especially men. Alice, a CEB leader, is convinced, however, that lack of time is just an excuse for most men. Having observed the difficulty of attracting men to the group, she discussed men's preference for using their leisure time for such activities as playing or watching football and watching television. In this respect, the strict morality of Pentecostal churches functions to create spare time, since few pursuits outside religious ones are sanctioned. Thus, for people who spend long hours at work, their free time tends to be dedicated only to religion. While Alice is correct in believing that a lack of time is often an excuse for men, men do not necessarily neglect their community responsibilities because of leisure activities. Several men are engaged in residents' associations. In the Alto José do Pinho association, for instance, there are more men than women.

Although most CEB members are retirees, the unemployed, or housewives, they are frequently individuals who by struggling hard have improved their lives; their life histories show that most, in fact, have been quite successful in obtaining a better economic situation for themselves and for their families. Alice is an example of such a person. After working in a factory for eighteen years, Alice decided to go back to school in order to find a better job. In her efforts to become a schoolteacher, she migrated to Recife. She not only became a schoolteacher with her own little school, but she also studied accounting and got a job teaching in another school. In addition, she built her own house. Nevertheless, Alice faced certain limitations in her ability to improve her life. The rewards for her education, for example, were relatively low compared with people from other class origins; and although her life improved, she never escaped the class poverty in which she began life.

Another example of self-improvement is the family of Maria Omar, a CEB member. Among all those interviewed, Maria Omar's family showed the most improvement economically. Although Maria Omar said she had always been a practicing Catholic and was engaged in the CEB activities of Alto José do Pinho, her husband, Antônio Omar, concerned himself with religion only after his retirement. In addition, Antônio does not go to the CEBs of his neighborhood, but prefers to participate with Maria in a middle-class Catholic religious movement— *Encontro de Casais com Cristo* (Meeting of Couples with Christ). Although husband and wife are now religious, Antônio was able to think about religion only after his retirement; before that, he was too busy trying to earn money. Antônio said that throughout his life, all his spare time was devoted to making extra money. For instance, for twelve years he worked as a waiter during Carnival. Antônio attributed his high motivation to work for his success. In his own words, *Muita gente não melhora por falta de esforço para trabalhar* ("Many people do not improve because they do not make the effort to work"). The life histories of both Antônio and Maria Omar thus reflect a highly motivated desire for improvement and success through hard work; this couple was able to buy a car and a telephone.[10] Maria Omar and Antônio were proud of their lives of hard work and the fact that two of their three sons studied law. The couple had also opened a small business from their home. Initially they had a bar, but later they turned it into a store where they sold vegetables and water; even today, though retired, they still sell fruits and popsicles. It is important, however, to note that Maria and Antônio Omar did not start at the lowest stratum of poverty; they never needed to pay rent because they inherited a small house from Maria Omar's mother. Although a very poor house made of clay and palm trees—almost a hut—it was later transformed by the couple into a middle-class house. This small inheritance may have been the initial advantage they needed for their success.

Aninha, another CEB member from Pernambuco, who owns a car and whose children go to college, also did not start at the lowest stratum of poverty. Her father, who had a stable job, was able to give her some education. Like all other CEB members, however, she faced very critical periods in her life. During one five-year spell, her husband was unemployed, and many economic problems surfaced because they had several young children to support. During this time, and with the help of her husband, Aninha sold goods at a market. She also told me about many other different things she did to support her family.

Margarida, who is from the state of Rio de Janeiro, also experienced very difficult times during her husband's illness. Nevertheless, she never needed to ask for help from outside her family. She got through the hard times by hard work, and she was aided by the fact that her brothers lived with them and could contribute to the family income.

Most of the CEB people interviewed had migrated to their area in order to obtain better jobs and economic situations. Most had succeeded in achieving this before joining the CEBs.

In contrast to Pentecostals, CEB members do not attribute their personal and family achievements to their religious affiliation and faith. Instead, they connect their religious activities to a general improvement of their neighborhood. Aninha, for instance, points to improvements in the infrastructure of neighborhood services as a result of her CEB work. She mentions the street pavement, street lighting, and garbage collection, among other improvements for which the CEB had worked. When some complained that their neighborhoods were not as developed as hers, she explained how all these improvements were the result of CEB struggle and organization. In Alto José do

Pinho, a poor neighborhood of Recife, Odete and Ernestina talked about how the new public school was obtained through CEB efforts. Maria Omar said that the struggle of the people from the Catholic church and especially the people from the CEBs are responsible for most of the improvements in their area; specifically, she told me about the struggle for better public transportation and a better water supply.

Most people interviewed seemed to have joined a CEB only after solving personal or family problems or after reaching a certain economic stability. Thus it seems that CEBs and Pentecostal churches seem to function to solve different problems and satisfy different needs. People from CEBs seem to have already improved their lives within the limitations of their class. Pentecostals, by contrast, tend to convert because of their difficulties in surviving poverty.

Nevertheless, there are exceptions in both groups. Maria José became a Pentecostal after having overcome her problems to survive. Among CEB members, Socorro is an exception. Her husband is both unemployed and an alcoholic, and she has endured many hardships. To support their three children, she works as a maid. Unable to pay rent, she attempted to build her own house in a squatter settlement. For Socorro, her CEB is not only the place to find emotional support in her fight for the land but also the place where she made contact with the Residents' Association, through which she hoped to have a job in a public day-care center about to be created in the area. In this instance, though it is an exception, the CEB is helping Socorro work on her individual problems. Other exceptions in CEBs were found among some of the elderly female members of the CEB in the Alto José do Pinho. Because of their age, they faced certain difficulties and were not as successful as some other CEB members. These elderly women participated in the religious activities of the groups but did not seem to understand or share the CEB worldview, their religious practices differing little from those of elderly Pentecostal women.

THE SOCIOECONOMIC SITUATION
OF AFRO-BRAZILIAN SPIRITISTS

In contrast to members of the Pentecostal churches and CEBs, Brazilians who practice Afro-Spiritism are of more diverse social origins. Umbanda, for instance, as Brown (1986) shows, is often a religion of middle-class people. Included among poor Umbanda adherents are those who have succeeded economically but have reached the limits of their class, as we saw earlier with members of the CEBs. Umbanda adherents, and Afro-Spiritists in general, also include those who are less successful but are nevertheless satisfied with their lot. These people develop a wide range of physical skills, rather than intellectual ones, and the limitations of their class to succeed are less clearly apparent than for people who are dissatisfied. Yet another situation is represented by people who can maintain only the same economic position as their family of origin. These individuals do not attain more, but simply have survived, as their parents did. Finally, among Afro-Spiritists there are those who experience a decline from the economic condition into which they were born. In contrast to most CEB members and Pentecostals, Afro-Spiritists become engaged in their religion while they are still working.

Socorrinho and José are examples of those whose lives have improved. Strongly motivated to improve, they have reached a higher intellectual and economic level than others beginning in the same circumstances; however, the limits to upward mobility in Brazil are all too clear from their experiences. For instance, after Socorrinho migrated to southern Brazil in order to find a better job, she made a considerable effort and completed the third grade of the *Ginásio* (this corresponds to the seventh grade of elementary school). In contrast, José began working at the age of thirteen, when he became a sailor. As he says, this was the fastest way for a poor boy to get ahead: "I went into the navy. At that time the navy was the only solution for poor boys from my town—either that or working in a warehouse without a future." Although both succeeded in obtaining more than their parents, their upward mobility was limited; they were not able to reach positions commensurate with their abilities. Despite her education, Socorrinho realized that the best occupation she could hope for was that of a maid, for which an education was not a requirement. For José, health problems forced him into early retirement. In contrast to members of the CEBs, Socorrinho and José were both attracted to the Umbanda, a form of Afro-Spiritism, while each struggled to succeed, not only economically but in terms of the psychological problems they were facing.

There are others from this religious group, such as João, Maria, Pinça, and Conceição, who also achieved a certain economic stability in relation to the rest of their community but developed fewer intellectual skills than José e Socorrinho and for that reason have a less clear notion of the structural limits to their upward mobility.

For instance, João was able to build five small houses in spite of being a Carnival club leader and the head of a household with a large number of children. João explained his ability to build the houses himself out of his savings because he did not drink. João also described himself as an extremely hard worker.

Maria, another highly active participant in a Carnival club, also described herself as a hard worker, explaining how she was able to build her own house, and how one of her daughters, who was able to study more than the other children, obtained a relatively good job, enabling her to help Maria. Although there is a belief that people who participate in Carnival spend almost all their money on it and therefore are unable to improve their economic condition, Maria and João show that Carnival organizers are frequently stereotyped as people who earn from the Carnival activities, which are supposed to be nonprofit. Both Maria and João say that their neighbors suspect them of taking money from the club; both deny the accusations. Pinça and

Conceição are further examples of Afro-Brazilian Spiritists who improved economically; each was able to send one of their children to college. In contrast, Graças and Luís are both examples of people with increasing difficulties. While Luís seems to be moving downward and has never had a stable job, Graça faces health problems.

To summarize, the economic situation of Afro-Brazilian Spiritists did not help in predicting their religious choices. In other words, no specific element or situation helps characterize Afro-Brazilian Spiritists as distinct from Brazilians belonging to other religions. What distinguishes the Afro-Spiritists are their subjective experiences. For example, they experience anguish and psychological conflict in their lives. They also face nonnatural experiences, such as seeing visions, hearing voices, or developing diseases with no scientific explanation. The Afro-Brazilian Spiritist people use their religion to search for the causes and to give meaning to these experiences and psychological sufferings. In this respect, their spiritual search is closer to that of the Pentecostals than that of the CEBs. For example, one interviewee, Agnaldo, said he became more involved in Afro-Spiritism when his wife became ill. Her illness created a family crisis. Agnaldo explained how they tried almost everything: how they went to a Protestant church; then they made Catholic *promessas*. Finally, they discovered that her problem was caused by spirits, and through some Afro-Spiritist rituals she recovered. Conceição, another of this group, also became involved with Afro-Spiritism when her nephew contracted a serious disease. Conceição began to receive spirits in an Afro-Spiritist center or, as she says, "She worked with spirits." And although she wants to stop these activities because they are very tiring, her family is pressuring her not to do so, explaining that when she stops and then something goes wrong, her husband and daughter will tell her that it is because she is no longer working with the spirits.

RELIGION AND IMPROVING
ECONOMIC CONDITIONS

In order to relate religion to an economic condition, a fourth category—people who are without any religious affiliation—must be analyzed. This heterogeneous group helps to identify the specific socioeconomic characteristics of each religious group. Although not officially engaged in any religion, some in this heterogeneous group still consider themselves religious. Some have a close relative, such as a child or a parent, who is active in one of the religious groups analyzed earlier; others have tried to join one of these groups or think about joining one in the future. These people are very diverse in their religious attitudes and preferences. In this group we have Zefinha, for instance, who says that she likes all religions, attends Protestant and Catholic churches equally, and has an Adventist son and a Spiritist daughter. As for Beto, although his sister and mother converted to the Baptist church and although he sympathizes with them in their beliefs and morality, he feels unable to follow them and convert.

Another example, Ilze, once tried to participate in the CEB in her area, but she gave it up after starting to work. She now considers herself to be a nonpracticing Catholic. Ilze also believes in Spiritism and has close relationships with people from many different religions. Ilze's mother and two of her sisters are converts to the Assembly of God; another sister is a Kardecist Spiritist; and Ilze's boy friend and his family practice a type of Afro-Brazilian Spiritism called Xangô. Another, Antônio Omar, discussed earlier, has only recently joined a Catholic group, having been religiously indifferent for most of his life. Others, such as Clemente and Faustina, say that although they were raised as practicing Catholics and believe that religion is very important, they do not belong to any religious group. Clemente says that he attended a CEB meeting once and did not like it because he was asked to speak and give his opinions. One of Clemente's daughters is affiliated with the Assembly of God.

None of these people shares a common economic pattern. Zefinha, Henrique, and Beto are economically successful; Faustina, Ilze, and Clemente are in economic trouble, each facing many financial difficulties. As among Afro-Brazilian Spiritists, the nonreligiously engaged are from all social strata within their poor areas. They have no specific characteristic in common to act as a predictor of their religious nonengagement. Religion therefore does not seem to be an important factor in predicting people's ability to improve economically. Equal numbers of people improved and did not improve among the different religious groups, as well as among those who belonged to no religious group.

Of the families in the different religious groups whose economic conditions improved, an important factor of that improvement seems to be family structure. For example, families headed by couples do better economically than single-parent families.[11] Parry Scott's (1988) data on another poor area in Recife support these conclusions.[12] In all cases of relative economic success, including those of Antônio, João, Henrique, Conceição, and Creuza, both parents are present in the family for a significant amount of time. A comparison of the life histories of Creuza and Neusa demonstrates this. Both women had similar experiences of facing the hardships of living in a large city after migrating from rural areas; each had an alcoholic husband, and each converted to Pentecostalism. Afterward, both were successful in converting their husbands as well. Shortly after Neusa's husband converted, however, he died, whereupon the material conditions of Neusa's family deteriorated rapidly. In contrast, Creuza's family's lot improved. In the two instances of families that were doing well economically but were headed by single women, Maria and Zefinha, the absence of the man as head of the household was relatively recent. The presence of a couple, however, does not assure a family's economic improvement. Most of the families headed by couples had no opportunity for economic improvement. Such was true in the families of Luís, an Afro-Spiritist, of Clemente, a traditional Catholic, and of Sebastião, Anésio, Metódio, and Manoel, all Pentecostals. Families headed by couples seem to have an advantage, if not for immediate economic improvement, at least for potential improvement. The presence of a couple, however, is not sufficient in itself; other elements for economic improvement factor into the mix.

Parry Scott (1988) notes that households headed by a single man fare equally as poorly as those headed by a single woman. He suggests that the presence of a couple, rather than gender, is the main factor to explain why a family is better off economically. Nevertheless, gender clearly limits the possibility of economic success. The better-paying, low-skill jobs—such as stevedore, mason, driver, and enlisting in the military—are not open to women. A low-skilled, hard-working woman might be a good laundress, but no matter how hard she works she will never make as much money as a similarly qualified male who works at the docks. And even with a higher level of education than their male counterparts, poor educated women tend to earn less. But although women do not have the same opportunities for economic improvement as men do, women seem to endure hardships better. One reason is that it is easier for women to avoid starvation, since they can work as housekeepers from an early age. For example, Ilze's mother's good fortune was to have female children because girls are able to earn money working as maids by age ten. In addition, women seem less prone to drinking and thus to alcoholism, and women are considered better able to save money.

Although religious affiliation does not allow us to predict a person's economic success or failure, socioeconomic condition helps predict whether a person is more likely to be attracted to CEB or Pentecostalism. As we saw earlier, the people in CEBs seem to face fewer economic problems at the time of their CEB engagement than Pentecostals at the time of their conversion. In effect, CEBs and Pentecostalism perform different economic roles in the lives of the poor. A comparative analysis of their strategies for coping with poverty may clarify their different appeal to people in Brazil.

STRATEGIES FOR COPING WITH POVERTY

I designate as "strategies" the means by which the poor cope with their poverty. These strategies involve the attitudes people develop to cope with a deprived situation, their everyday actions and behaviors in the struggle to survive and improve their lot, and the creative and manifold utilization of their limited resources. According to David Maybury Lewis, strategies are the different social practices by which people try to escape the fate of their structural positions.[13] Although the success and nature of these strategies are limited by the structure in which they occur, the strategies do vary, their diversity revealing the relative autonomy of the culture.

As manifold as the many states of poverty, every strategy by the poor to extricate themselves is an attempt to obtain extra goods and income, differing only in the nature of the attempt. In order to analyze and understand these strategies for coping with poverty it may be convenient to classify them according to the three basic means used: the material, the political, and the cultural nature of these strategies.

Material strategies directly create goods and income for the poor and are characterized by the economic or material means used to do so. For example, the production of new goods, the creation of new kinds of jobs, the organization by the poor of self-help groups, or merely a request for goods or money are all material strategies based on different material or economic means.

Political strategies are the simple exchange of votes for goods or money as well as the more complex creation of a political organization for demanding improvements. Cultural strategies, finally, are the beliefs, symbols, and attitudes used by and for the poor as their motivations to struggle to survive or to overcome their poverty. These cultural elements are grounded in the individuals' psychological and subjective experiences. The behaviors that result from new cultural elements and subjective experiences may be very diverse. For instance, cultural strategies could include the beliefs that motivate individuals to be upwardly mobile, but they could also be beliefs that foster political participation by the poor. In reality, these three kinds of strategies are interdependent and interconnected; their distinction is for analytical purposes only.

This analysis requires two additional but parallel classifications of the three basic strategies, based on different criteria. The first criterion of any given strategy is the test of the logic of its relation to the broad economic and political system (Clark 1988). Some strategies, for example, merely follow the rules of the system and do not foster its transformation; they even may be functional to the system's growth and contribute to its success. Other strategies may oppose or threaten the established system by generating an internal conflict or by creating an alternative system.

The second criterion involves the question of who is the major actor in the strategy. In other words, strategies differ according to whom they benefit and by whom they are organized. Some strategies may be employed by an individual or a family simply for its own benefit; other strategies may be organized by an interest group or local organization, such as a religious group, leisure club, or class association for the mutual benefit of the group only; or strategies may be envisioned as a help to all poor and needy people equally. Thus, strategies may be individual, group, or collectively oriented, and each material, political, and cultural strategy may differ in its relationship to the logic of the system and according to whom it benefits, the tendency to adopt different strategies depending very much on the individual or group's worldviews. For example, as a result of their different values, religions vary in relation to the strategies they tend to encourage.

All behaviors, however, that might be considered strategies for coping with poverty may not be consciously perceived as such. Some behaviors may have a very different motivation and intention, and coping with poverty may be nothing more than the unintended consequence of these behaviors. Thus, what makes behaviors strategies for coping with poverty is not necessarily their explicit, conscious motivation and goal, but the actual results achieved by them. For example, we find behaviors analyzed here whose motivations are solely religious, but whose consequence is material. In order to escape poverty, people need first to survive it; someone who is successful in overcoming poverty by definition must first survive it. Thus strategies that help people to endure poverty and those that help them to overcome it are part of the same process. Not all who survive poverty, however, are also able to overcome it.

In order to understand how each religion develops and ascribes meaning to a certain strategy, and why some religions are more popular than others, we need to understand and to compare each religious worldview. That is the subject of the next chapter.

CHAPTER III

A Comparison of Religious Worldviews

One Wednesday evening, a CEB meeting was scheduled at Aniceto's house in Alto José do Pinho in Recife, but only Aniceto's family and a close neighbor, Socorro, showed up. One of the last chapters of a popular *telenovela* (a Brazilian form of soap opera) was being shown on television, said Aniceto's wife, explaining the absence of the others even as she herself turned on the television set. Neither Aniceto's family nor Socorro seemed disappointed at the evening's poor turnout. This is a sharp contrast between the appeal of Pentecostal churches, and the religious commitment of their members, and that of the CEBs.

Despite their significance as a new social movement in Brazil, the Catholic Base Communities (CEBs) are numerically a minor religious phenomenon compared to other religious movements (Daudelin 1990). Catholic priests working with CEBs in poor areas have observed the relatively low attendence of their parishioners at celebrations and Masses in comparison with those of more traditional religious orientation or with services in Pentecostal churches. One Catholic priest from Baixada Fluminense, a poor area in the state of Rio de Janeiro, noted that the Catholic church was a minority in this area, while in Recife another progressive Catholic priest mentioned that Mass said by a traditionally oriented priest in a neighboring parish was better attended than his own. He suggested that people have difficulty accepting the participative style of the progressive Catholic church and observed that whereas in his own parish there are fifty baptisms a year, in the traditional parishes there are fifty a week. Both progressive priests noted the difficulty of recruiting new members to CEBs and the striking growth of Pentecostalism. This growth intrigues not only Catholic priests but Protestant pastors from non-Pentecostal denominations as well.

A comparison of Pentecostalism and CEB worldviews with Afro-Brazilian Spiritism and nonromanized Brazilian Catholicism, here also referred to as folk Catholicism, can further our understanding of why CEBs have less appeal to the poor than Pentecostalism does and can clarify how each religious outlook supports and legitimizes different strategies for coping with poverty.[1]

Pentecostalism and CEBs can both be considered popular religions in that they have been accepted by the poor; however, in order to understand the process of cultural change, it is useful to distinguish them from traditional Brazilian popular religion. While both new worldviews are numerical minorities, they propose to transform the view of the majority of the population, indicating that the groups perceive themselves as outside mainstream Brazilian popular culture, rather than a variant thereof. And in fact, both movements originated elsewhere. Pentecostalism arrived from abroad. The founders of the *Assembléia de Deus do Brasil* (Assembly of God of Brazil) were Swedes, and that of the *Congregação Cristã do Brasil* (Christian Congregation of Brazil) was an Italian. They had all become Pentecostals in the United States, and as such are frequently seen as outsiders. Although the CEBs originated in Latin America, the CEB perspective can also be considered alien to the poor because it emerged, not from their experiences, but from middle-class intellectual thought.[2] CEBs are the result of an intentional pastoral work by church agents, most of whom are well educated. Thus, both worldviews originated from experiences other than those of the Brazilian poor (Adriance 1986; Benedetti 1988). Although alien in terms of nationality, Pentecostals are not so in terms of social class. Pentecostalism emerged originally among the black American poor (Anderson 1979; Rolim 1985). And Daniel Berg, the founder of the Assembly of God in Brazil, was from a working-class family in Sweden and became a foundryman in the United States.[3]

Despite their different social origins and contrasting views, Pentecostalism and CEBs share the idea that traditional folk religion must be changed. They aim to modify not only the way people relate to God, to others, and to the world, but their whole way of thinking. The aspects they attempt to change are different, however, as is revealed by the distinctive names each uses to designate its attempt to transform people's minds. Pentecostals deem their task a *missionary work*, while CEB pastoral agents think of their activities as *consciousness raising* or *popular education* (Duarte 1983). These terms indicate contrasting ideas of what needs to be changed. Missionary work is basically religious. It emphasizes the transformation of values and moral assumptions and views the ethics of potential converts as morally inferior. Educational work, in contrast, places emphasis on the transformation of cognitive assumptions and considers the person to be educated as lacking in cognitive competence. Thus Pentecostals emphasize the transformation of folk reli-

gion's normative assumptions or values, while CEBs propose
to change its cognitive presuppositions.[4]

The concept of popular culture or popular religion is frequently found in the discourse of CEB pastoral agents and
priests, as well as in liberation theology literature. In Pentecostal publications and sermons, the concept never appears.
This indicates an affinity between the Pentecostals' worldview
and that of popular culture, in contrast to the worldview of pastoral agents, whose concept of popular culture demonstrates
their standpoint as outsiders from the poor people's cultural
universe. Further, Pentecostals hold no general idea of culture,
but deem their habits concerning leisure, dress, and the like the
"doctrine" of their religion, while adopting a literal interpretation of the Bible. Their religious faith and cultural habits cannot be separated.[5] In contrast, although less common among
CEB members, the idea of culture is fundamental to the view
taught by CEBs because it allows a "contextualization" of the
Bible, that is, the adaptation of Bible teachings to everyday
life, as opposed to a literal reading. CEB literature stresses the
importance of accepting folk religions and integrating popular
religious language into CEB experience (Libânio 1986).[6]

A COMPARISON OF RELIGIOUS
ASSUMPTIONS

Both CEBs and Pentecostalism propose a break with some of
folk religion's most important assumptions, beginning with
those related to religious symbols. When CEBs introduce the
concept of culture and their idea of contextualization, they
are assuming that symbols and rituals are mere cultural ap-
pearances, rather than the core of the religious message. CEBs
break with popular religion by affirming that religious symbols are relative and that true religion deals with principles and
ethics. Pentecostals share this assumption and are very critical
of the emphasis that folk religion places on symbols, rituals,

and icons. But they prefer to deny popular religion's symbols and rituals, rather than try to relativize them. They attempt to strip away all symbols from their churches, preferring sponta- neous rather than formal prayers and austere temples and ritu- als. Their underlying normative assumption is that "symbols are bad."[7]

CEB pastoral agents assume that folk religion adopts the symbolism of the dominant class (Betto 1984) and that the use of this alien symbolism can destroy the liberating power of the Christian message. Theirs is a rational concept that con- siders symbols not as real phenomena, but as representations.[8] They propose a new religious language utilizing symbolic ele- ments from the daily life of the poor. One example of this, described by Friar Betto (1984, 19), is to substitute the bread used at Mass with consecrated *cuscuz*, a popular and cheap food made of corn. Although these are attempts to adapt religion to local culture, perhaps their greatest effect is that people be- come disenchanted with traditional symbols and come to face the relativity of their beliefs and culture. Instead of overcoming ethnocentrism, these experiences strip symbols of their mythi- cal power by reducing them to mere representations. This ex- plains why, despite their docility regarding the religious au- thority of priests, the poor can react negatively to some of the proposed changes. For example, John Burdick (1990), ob- served a community that rejected their priest's idea of celebrat- ing a feast day of Our Lady by crowning an elderly woman of the community rather than an image of Our Lady.

Both Pentecostals and CEB members share the idea that reli- gion is an actualization of God's plan for humanity; they believe in Providence. Religion is more than a simple relationship be- tween the human being and God; it requires human acceptance of and engagement in God's plan. Behind the idea that God has a plan lies a linear conception of history offering ground for a universal ethic. CEB pastoral agents recognize the im- portance of substituting popular culture's circular concept of history with this linear concept, which leaves room for social change.[9] Further, acceptance of, or participation in, God's plan requires an adoption of ethical behavior, which for Pentecostals implies obedience to a universal moral ethic in private life and for CEBs implies a commitment to a social ethic in the public sphere.

The idea of God's plan is also implicit in the terms that each group uses for its religious activity. Pentecostals refer to the *Obra* (task) to which they are committed, while CEB people often speak of the *Caminhada* (walk) in which they participate. Both terms include the idea of a goal to be reached in the future. In fact, the emphasis given to God's plan is a religious novelty introduced by Pentecostalism and CEBs, for in the tradition of Afro-Brazilian Spiritism, there is no concept of Providence or God's plan for humanity, no plan to which one must be committed, and no linear conception of history. This explains why, in general,[10] Afro-Brazilian Spiritism does not offer universal ethical principles, nor does it relate ethical behavior to religious activities. Consequently, rituals and symbols play a more important role than do the universal principles of ethics and morality; in this respect, folk Catholicism in Brazil draws close to Afro-Spiritism.

There are certain differences between CEB and Pentecostal ideas of what God's plan is. These differences do not lie, as Rolim (1980) suggested, in opposition between the "other-worldliness" of the Pentecostal plan and the "innerworldliness" of the CEB idea, for in both views, the "otherworld" and this world are very much interrelated and interdependent. God's plan begins in this life, where both CEBs and Pentecostals aim to transform people's behavior, rather than draw them away from worldly affairs. Thus, CEB and Pentecostal views are certainly oriented to this world. In addition, for Pentecostals, God is quite active in this world, punishing the sinful and recompensing the virtuous. Pentecostals find obvious signs of God's blessing and spiritual salvation. They frequently offer accounts of healing where conversion resulted in improved health, as exemplified by Creuza, who interpreted her preconversion disease and suffering as God's punishment for the unseemly way in which she had treated members of the Assembly of God. For Pentecostals, God's plan is confirmed and supported by prophesies, cures, and miracles experienced in daily life. In contrast, the CEB view does not recognize miracles or supernatural occurrences in everyday lives, nor does it assume any relationship between miracles and God's plan. God does not use miracles to help human beings carry out his plan; instead, he uses human beings and relies on their abilities. Thus, the difference between the Pentecostal and CEB idea of God's plan lies not in their otherworldly or innerworldly orientations but in their assumptions of how God's plan can be carried out in this world.

The Pentecostal idea that God's plan or Providence must rely on supernatural means is quite plausible in popular culture, which is grounded in the assumption that the supernatural can be experienced in everyday life. For both Pentecostals and Afro-Brazilian Spiritists, miracles and supernatural experiences are commonplace, and members of both groups have visions, hear prophesies, and perform supernatural cures. Even when not specifically asked about miracles or supernatural events, nearly all the Pentecostals and Afro-Brazilian Spiritists interviewed mentioned such experiences in their everyday lives, an element most uncommon in interviews of CEB members and pastoral agents. In fact, CEB pastoral agents avoid discussions of miracles and other supernatural events and hold a different concept of a living God. One CEB priest confessed how difficult it was for him when he was asked to bless a sick child in order to cure him, for he believed that his blessing would do little to solve health problems, whereas for most Brazilian poor, a blessing could help as much as any scientific cure. In comparison to that of popular culture, as well as to that of Pentecostals, CEB pastoral agents have a very secular and rational worldview.

As a rule, Pentecostalism and Brazilian folk religions share the same cognitive universe but disagree in their normative presuppositions (Cook 1985). While Afro-Brazilian Spiritists accept all supernatural facts without making value judgments, Pentecostals believe that only miracles performed by the Holy Ghost are legitimate; all other spirits who have the power to perform miracles are devils. In their interviews, Pentecostals made mention of miracles performed by the Evil One. Neusa believed that the strange fever she had had before her baptism was a result of her husband's Afro-Brazilian Spiritist activities and was caused by the devil. "Liberation," for Pentecostals, means "to be free from the power of bad spirits," and they strongly fight Afro-Brazilian Spiritists who, they believe, are able to perform miracles without the aid of the Holy Ghost. Afro-Brazilian Spiritism is met with antagonism by Pentecostals, who acknowledge its supernatural power, and with condescension by CEB pastoral agents, who, in general, do not believe in Afro-Spiritism. But this tolerance is not always shared by CEB members. Ernestina, a CEB member from Pernambuco, referred to Xangô as witchcraft, and when asked about the presence of Afro-Brazilian Spiritist groups in his area, Otacílio, a CEB member and active participant of *Pastoral da Terra* in Rio de Janeiro, referred to these groups as "weeds among the wheat."

The second aspect that differentiates CEB and Pentecostal notions of God's plan is that in the CEB view this plan relates to community life, rather than personal experience. The CEB view assumes the individual's dependence on his society or group and therefore does not emphasize personal morality or individual transformation in the process of working out God's plan in this world. Instead, the CEB proposal is an attempt to build a community identity for the poor (Macedo 1986), which is absent in other popular religions. The creation of this identity is an intentional break with popular religions by pastoral agents, a rupture related to certain cognitive and value assumptions about the political life. The Pentecostal idea of God's plan requires no elaboration of class identity; it is therefore more plausible in popular culture than the CEB version.

THE ECONOMIC CULTURE
OF EACH VIEW

Assumptions about Poverty

CEBs and Pentecostals place the same emphasis on economic and material life as do folk religions. Both can be considered "innerworld" oriented, in the Weberian sense; thus neither disagrees with popular religions. Both consider poverty something to be avoided and assume that the economic improvement of one's material condition is a legitimate goal in life. Nevertheless, each proposes a different approach to the struggle for material improvement and attributes a different meaning to it because each holds different cognitive and normative assumptions about poverty.

Although CEBs consider the poor to be God's chosen people, they teach these people to reject their poverty and strive for a better life. The CEB perspective rejects not only absolute poverty but also relative poverty or social inequality, which is interpreted as a consequence of social sin, identified with class exploitation. To combat inequality and poverty is to combat this sin, a logic very clearly expressed in CEB literature and in the discourse of CEB pastoral agents.

Pentecostals have a different way of rejecting poverty. They emphasize that the fundamental goal of a person's life is the salvation of his soul, but they acknowledge the relationship of spiritual salvation to material life. This idea is explicit in a text used in the Assembly of God Sunday school, which affirms: "One cannot have a spiritual and moral life without financial responsibility; for this reason, financial (economic) sciences are very important in all Christian homes."[11] Pentecostals are little concerned with social inequality and relative poverty but perceive and reject absolute poverty. They consider the comparison of people's economic advantages as a sign of envy. Absolute poverty is often interpreted as the consequence of an irresponsible life, for God usually blesses a good spiritual life with economic advantages. Despite their belief in the individual's responsibility for his or her material conditions, Pentecostals acknowledge that this responsibility is only partial because they also assume that God has a plan for each individual. This notion of Providence relieves the stress of those who face economic problems and gives meaning to their suffering. To identify the cause of one's problems as other than God's will or the consequences of individual sin implies a diminishing of God's power.

Pentecostalism includes a strong work ethic, for it assumes that God protects the hard worker and that, through work, one can attain economic stability and success. This assumption is quite different from that of folk Catholicism, Afro-Brazilian Spiritism, and CEBs, which also value work and the hard worker but deny the relationship between hard work and economic improvement (Cardoso 1978). Afro-Brazilian Spiritism holds that one's economic improvement depends less on working hard than on having a "strong saint" to protect and help. CEB members believe that the hard-working poor person rarely receives the salary he or she deserves, nor can that person always find a job. Unlike Pentecostalism, therefore, folk Catholicism, Afro-Brazilian Spiritism, and CEBs do not promote a work ethic. CEB textbooks and meetings discuss salary and job options, rather than individual workers' morality. The word *work* is normally used as a synonym for *job*, and it is a personal goal to strive for, like homeownership and children's education.[12] The CEB perspective does not attribute religious meaning or motivation to individual economic behavior because it assumes that poor isolated individuals cannot do much to improve their economic life. Unlike other elements of the CEB view analyzed here, this idea is shared by CEB members and pastoral agents alike. CEBs seem to attract people whose personal experiences of the impossibility of individual improvement have already brought them close to the CEB outlook. Benedita, a CEB member from Alto do Carneiro, Recife, for instance, clearly defended this point when explaining her daughter's job situation. The daughter had spent many years in school but was unable to get a good job at fair wages. In contrast, Pentecostalism and folk religion see economics as an individual problem and do not normally consider community organization as a solution.

The Value of Giving

Poor people depend very much on one another's support in order to survive adverse economic conditions; thus they develop and value their neighborhood and kinship networks. Community mutual help networks are a value of popular culture and not a novelty introduced by CEBs, as Castro (1987) and Petrini (1984) suggest. The existence and esteem of mutual help among kin and neighbors, however, does not necessarily indicate the existence of a community identity or an identity of the poor, such as CEBs attempt to create. Poor people help one another because they have needs, not because they identify with one another. What CEBs do is reinforce this value and attribute religious meaning to it. In their view, economic equality is one of God's goals for humanity, and helping each other and the poorest is an important part of their religious ethic.

Traditional folk religions also value the distribution of economic goods. Xangô (a traditional branch of Afro-Brazilian Spiritism) emphasizes the distribution of food in their services, and no one can be refused a portion. The "father [or mother] of saint," a title applied to religious leaders of these groups, shows power and wealth by giving away as much as possible (Brandão 1987; Motta 1983). Thus, the meaning and goal of giving are quite different for Spiritists and CEBs. Afro-Spiritists give, not because they aim for equality, but to show power and generate dependence. It is a self-serving, ostentatious generosity, for their giving demonstrates de facto inequality and symbolically reinforces it.

In contrast, Pentecostalism does not confer any religious significance onto giving. Pentecostal churches do not propose to help their poorest members, and members do not expect help from the church. They expect help only from God because they assume that he alone is able to give anything. He can reveal a job or make one friend help another. Generally, Pentecostals do not beg or even ask others for help (Gomes 1985). During one Sunday school class I observed, women were taught that they must never ask their husbands for anything; the religious woman prays to God. The teacher said that she never asked her husband for anything. When in need, she would approach her husband by saying, "Levi, I am praying to God to get a new blender." God might then touch her husband and make him buy it. This aversion to asking for help and things, coupled with the idea that only God can give, suggests that Pentecostals share with Afro-Brazilian Spiritists the cognitive assumption that people give to show superiority and to dominate the recipients of their gifts. They assume that giving leads, not to equality, but to dependence, and that the only good dependence is dependence on God. Therefore, these views once again share a common cognitive presupposition, while differing in their value judgments. Despite their different values, however, in order to survive Pentecostals continue to participate in different community networks of mutual help (Novaes 1985; Page 1984). Nevertheless, they interpret all help received as sent from God.

Religious Spending

Although Pentecostals do not attribute any religious meaning to generosity toward the poor, they are generous to their churches, to which they usually tithe and give extra offerings. Like Pentecostals, Afro-Brazilian Spiritist centers are also supported by their members and stress the value of religious spending. For both Afro-Brazilian Spiritism and folk Catholicism, expenditures for sacred goods are considered legitimate, even when these expenses are relatively high, such as those involved in some Afro-Brazilian Spiritist rituals. There is a striking contrast between the poverty of the community and the high cost of Xangô group rituals (Brandão 1987; Motta 1983). Pentecostals differ from Afro-Brazilian Spiritists in their patterns of religious consumption. Unlike the Afro-Brazilian Spiritists, they spend less on rituals and more on instrumental goods, such as the construction of temples, the payment of salaries, and the purchase of sound systems. This contrasting pattern of religious consumption reveals the different value placed on symbolism and ritual within each religion. It is also important to notice that Pentecostals contribute to an institution—the church—that is generally independent of any specific person and is not owned by anyone.[13] Spiritist centers are not normally independent institutions, but someone's property, and members' gifts will benefit the owner of the center: a specific "mother [or father] of saint."[14]

In contrast to these groups, the progressive Catholic church tries to avoid spending money on rituals or for church construction. CEB pastoral agents believe that poor people should spend their money trying to improve their lives, rather than on sacred goods. They consider that Pentecostal churches and Afro-Brazilian Spiritist centers are exploiting the poor by asking for money. This value judgment indicates their secularized outlook, which marks a crucial rupture of the CEB perspective from popular culture.

THE POLITICAL CULTURE
OF EACH VIEW

CEBs represent an intentional break with the authoritarian, centralist, and personalist aspects of Brazilian political culture (Mainwaring and Viola 1987). CEB pastoral agents have the explicit goal of changing the political behavior of the poor in two fundamental ways: through the creation of a class identity that will allow the poor to become political actors, and by the adoption of a radical style of democracy with grassroots, or "base," participation. As mentioned earlier, the CEB conception of God's plan presumes the existence of a collective identity, which the CEBs intend to help create. Although poor people know that they are poor and perceive that their situation is the very opposite of the rich, the mere recognition of poverty does not generate a unified identity. As a group, there are multiple identities among the poor, which are not related primarily to their economic situation. The definition of an identity does not depend solely on cognitive assumptions or on the perception of sharing similar characteristics; it depends on value judgments. People adopt identities based on the characteristics they value most. Therefore, the CEB attempt to create an identity for the poor is not only a break with popular culture's cognitive assumptions but also a break with popular culture's values.

In order to create an identity as "the poor," poor people must not only perceive that they have similar interests as a result of their economic situation but they must have common characteristics. For that reason, CEBs try to raise poor people's self-esteem and define the poor as God's chosen people. CEBs tend toward an ecumenical posture, instead of stressing their religious affiliation and identity. In contrast, popular culture stresses the differences among the poor (Zaluar 1985). Most people prefer to be identified as something other than the negative stereotype of the poor. This preference for a classless basis of identity is present in Afro-Brazilian Spiritist, traditional Catholic, and Pentecostal views and hinders development of the class identity that CEBs try so hard to create. CEB pastoral agents are critical of this preference and believe that, within a religion, the absence of a unified identity of the poor leads to an individualistic idea of God's plan and to the adoption of apolitical religion, which is restricted to private life. For pastoral agents such as Betto (1984), these private religions are part of the dominant ideology and must be transformed. For their part, Pentecostals are unconcerned with the transformation of politics; they assume that religion is apolitical and does not specifically address the poor. Although Pentecostals also create a new identity, it is one that further differentiates the poor. Pentecostal identity is independent of economic situation and does not break from any cognitive or normative assumptions of popular culture.

The most important political consequence of a collective identity is that it defines the political alliances people will establish. CEB pastoral agents believe that a new identity of the poor can unify, strengthen, and transform them into an independent political action group. They believe the poor should enter into horizontal political alliances with other poor people, rather than into vertical alliances through which they can be manipulated. In this respect, Pentecostals share with Afro-Brazilian Spiritists a preference for vertical political alliances (Stoll 1986). They assume that the poor do not always share the same interests and that poor groups may need the support of stronger allies.

The second CEB proposal is that of participatory democracy. The authority of CEB leaders is limited by the votes of its members, all decisions are submitted for the community's approval, and members take turns filling different functional and power positions (Castro 1987).

The political praxis in Afro-Brazilian Spiritist centers is just the opposite, with power concentrated in the hands of the center's owner. Centers are not owned by the community of members; instead, members belong to the center. In general, Afro-Brazilian Spiritist leaders even own the houses in which meetings and rituals take place. The overriding value is obedience, and members do not participate in running the center. José, an Afro-Brazilian Spiritist leader from Rio de Janeiro, admits that most of the time he acts as a little dictator. Pentecostals value obedience as much as adherents of folk religion and popular culture do. They claim that all authority comes from God and must be respected, and several authors have pointed out the authoritarian aspect of Pentecostalism and the absence of democratic participation in community decisions.[15] These authors suggest that Pentecostals follow popular political traditions and assume the values and beliefs of popular political culture. It appears, however, that despite being as authoritarian as folk religions and popular culture as a whole, Pentecostalism fosters a different kind of authority legitimation. The authority of pastors is conferred not only by their personal charisma and style but also by the institution they belong to and by their ethical behavior. Pastors must follow the "doctrine," or religious ethic; otherwise, church members may disobey them (Aubrée 1984). Pentecostals may also disrespect secular authorities when these authorities stray from God's law. In contrast to the person-based authoritarianism of Afro-Brazilian Spiritism and popular culture, the law-based authoritarianism of Pentecostalism allows members to disobey and criticize authorities. In this respect, the Pentecostal view and political praxis represent a partial break from that of popular culture.

In contrast to Pentecostalism, the CEB view proposes a total break with the political assumptions of popular culture when it questions the value of obedience to leaders and leaders' right to make decisions without consulting community members. Nevertheless, the CEB attempt to put its democratic principles into practice in everyday decisions faces limitations. The first problem CEBs come up against is that it is very difficult to change political behavior.[16] Several pastoral agents interviewed observed the authoritarian tendency of certain CEB leaders, who monopolized the decision-making process instead of listening to other people's opinions. Pastoral agents deemed them *minipadres* (minipriests). Another limitation of the CEBs results from the fact that CEBs are not autonomous but are still part of the hierarchical Catholic church, even though their very existence is an attempt to change this stratified and authoritarian structure. A third limitation can be found in the cognitive and value assumptions of the concept of participatory democracy. Radical participatory democracy assumes that all competing opinions in a group can find equally competent verbal defenders; thus, the ability to convince people verbally is greatly valued. These assumptions and values are not shared by traditional folk religion in Brazil. Afro-Brazilian Spiritism and folk Catholicism are not verbal, or "logophilic" (Turner 1975). This fact can be observed by noting the minor role words play in Afro-Brazilian Spiritism (Motta 1983). Therefore it takes some time for most poor people to feel at ease at CEB meetings, where everyone must speak. Neci, for example, a retired black maid, said that she could not participate in CEBs because of her age and because she did not know how to express herself. Clemente, a retired white rural worker, also mentioned having given up attendance at CEB meetings because people were always asking him to speak. Pastoral agents are aware of this problem, and the development of poor people's verbal skills is a real goal of CEB popular education. Consequently, despite all the voting processes for decision making in these groups, theirs is still a relative democracy because of the uneven distribution of verbal skills between pastoral agents and ordinary CEB members or leaders.

This asymmetry is less pronounced among Pentecostals because most of their leaders are from the same social milieu as the members. Nevertheless, in a different way from that of the CEBs, Pentecostalism also values the use of words and the development of verbal skills, particularly in preaching. Neusa described how a pastor's preaching had influenced her decision "to accept Jesus" and join the Assembly of God. She had been very moved by the pastor's message that Jesus came to relieve the oppressed. Roxinha was equally enchanted by what she referred to as "the pastor's eloquent words." Among Pentecostals, the development of verbal skills is a consequence of proselytism and missionary work, whereas in CEBs it occurs through debates and decision-making meetings.

Pentecostalism is more logophilic than Afro-Brazilian Spiritism, but is not as logophilic as are CEBs. Pentecostalism offers the trancelike experience of receiving the Holy Ghost, which places it somewhere between the Afro-Brazilian religion and CEBs in relation to the emphasis on the "logos" and on speaking or debating ability as a means of religious expression.

PENTECOSTALISM, CEBS, AND
THE RATIONALITY OF RELIGION

The following analysis suggests some explanations as to why Pentecostalism is advancing so much faster than CEBs among the Brazilian poor. First, Pentecostalism is not as secularized as the CEBs; it lies closer to popular culture and religion by assuming most of their cognitive assumptions about the supernatural. The CEB view represents a sharp break with folk religions because it attempts, through a process of consciousness raising, to redefine important cognitive assumptions about these religions and culture. Despite the pastoral agents' intentions to incorporate and reinforce some of the values of popular culture, such as the sharing of goods and a high opinion of religion, there is no continuity between the CEB message and the values of popular culture. The discontinuity in their cognitive presuppositions implies a discontinuity in their normative assumptions. These secularizing or rationalizing elements of the CEB view are implicit in its assumption that religious truth can be known not only by revelation but also by rational analysis and theoretical knowledge. Pastoral agents believe that rational analysis can separate the truth from the dominant ideology, and they propose popular education to give people the theoretical tools for this analysis. Thus they believe that religious people should study more and be more intellectual in order to develop a deeper faith and better understand the religious message. Consequently, they value education highly (Macedo 1986). Pentecostalism is rationalizing because in it the development of religious experience requires not only that individuals experience the Holy Ghost but also that they study the Bible and understand it rationally. This is clearly true for the Assembly of God, whose numbers of seminaries are growing in Brazil. In contrast, in order to be a religious leader of Afro-Brazilian Spiritism, one need not have any specific intellectual preparation or rational knowledge. The initiation required is more frequently in terms of physical experiences, such as eating special foods or living in a forest for a few days.[17]

The higher degree of secularization of the CEB view probably explains why some committed CEB members have left CEBs to become involved in political movements that have no religious connotation. Most of the authors who have analyzed this problem (Betto 1984; Fernandes 1985) explain it from a macrosocial perspective, claiming that the political democratization (the so-called *Abertura*) of Brazil has allowed for the development of new social movements to compete with CEBs. There may be a complementary explanation from the perspective of the individual religious experience. People who adopt the secularizing view of CEBs may weaken their faith and become less concerned with religion. This secularizing view may diminish their traditional high esteem of religion. Therefore, CEBs live the paradox of rationality pointed out by Weber in relation to the Protestant ethic. If people accept the CEB view, as proposed by pastoral agents, in the long run CEBs will lose their religious power for political mobilization. Certain priests and pastoral agents have already noticed this and are concerned, among other nonsecular problems, with deepening the faith of CEB participants. According to an Italian progressive Catholic priest who works in Pernambuco, some CEB people lose their faith when they become involved in politics because they lack religious education. He therefore teaches the Bible to his parishioners in classes that are not intended to give people faith, for "people have more faith than the priest," as he says, but to offer intellectual or rational support for their faith.

The second explanation for the success of Pentecostal churches is the fact that these churches are almost exclusively made up of poor people. Many of their leaders are people from equally empoverished backgrounds with no university-level education. Pentecostal churches may defend authoritarian values, but they offer a fairly egalitarian relationship between pastors and ordinary members. In contrast, CEB pastoral agents are much more educated than CEB members are, and despite the democratic values of CEBs, their democratic experience is limited by the unequal verbal competence between members and pastoral agents. The Catholic church opts for the poor because it is not a church of the poor. Pentecostal churches do not opt for the poor because they are already a poor people's church. And that is why poor people are choosing them.

CHAPTER IV

Material Strategies for Coping with Poverty

Because houses in poor Brazilian neighborhoods are not sturdily built, each year after strong rains many poor families are left homeless. During my research in Alto José do Pinho, one homeless family was living in the social hall that belonged to the Assembly of God and another was living in the hall next to the Catholic church chapel that served as the neighborhood's CEB meeting place. Both halls were designed to hold meetings, wedding parties, and other social activities. The displaced families lived there only temporarily, while they arranged to find new homes. Their use of the space illustrates how religious groups and institutions can help people cope with the immediate problems of poverty. It also shows some distinctions among the two religious groups.

Whereas the family living in the Assembly of God hall was that of a Pentecostal religious leader, the people living in the Catholic chapel were not participants in any religious activities of the Catholic church. This suggests that among Pentecostals the degree of integration into the church affects the possibilities for its members to obtain occasional aid from the church. In this respect, aid from Pentecostal churches differs from aid offered by the CEBs and the Catholic church.

Although most religious groups create and distribute material resources to the poor, they differ in the amount of aid they offer and in the procedures employed to distribute such aid. Generally, a religious group gives material goods in one of two ways. It pays people who perform religious work, or it offers aid to the poorest and most needy. The performance of each religious group as a source of income and an instrument for material survival depends largely on its value assumptions and worldviews, which were discussed in Chapter 3.

MATERIAL SUPPORT OFFERED BY PENTECOSTAL CHURCHES

In contrast to the Catholic church, historical Protestant churches, and Spiritist groups, Pentecostal churches generally do not, as institutions, provide relief for the poor. In the neighborhood of Alto José do Pinho, in Recife, the Assembly of God does not offer any material aid to the poorest people in the area or to the poorest members of the church. Members can help one another, as we discuss in the section about networks of support, but the church itself does not offer any financial assistance. This is also the practice of that neighborhood's other Pentecostal church the *Igreja do Evangelho Quadrangular*. This lack of material aid can be explained in part by the poverty of the members of these religious groups. In fact, I have observed that some richer Pentecostal churches, such as the Assembly of God churches of Jacarezinho, a large *favela* in Rio de Janeiro, and Cachoeira de Macacu, a small city in the state of Rio de Janeiro, distribute soup to the poorest in the area and give weekly grocery supplies to the church's neediest members. The pastor of Cachoeira de Macacu's church says the ladies' group in his church is engaged in social work activities.

But the poverty of the members of these religious groups only partially explains the absence of institutional charity. Other groups, such as the Baptist church and CEBs, whose members are also very poor, refer to the practice of collecting a *feirinha* (food for one week) for those in need. Another explanation for the behavior of the Pentecostal churches of Alto José do Pinho may come from the Pentecostal attitude toward charity. Despite the limitations and infrequency of help offered by the Baptist church and CEBs, members of these groups emphasize charitable works. This may indicate that aid to the poor has more religious meaning for Baptist and CEB people than for Pentecostals.

The absence of value placed on the practice of charity by these churches and their individual members is noticed and criticized by outsiders, particularly by those who are related to Umbanda, who have been severely antagonized by Pentecostals. Graças, an *Umbandista*, says, "There are many mean 'believers' (Protestants) who do not give at least a Good Morning." Ilze, who considers herself a nonpracticing Catholic, compares the Pentecostals (*crentes*, or "believers") with Spiritists and says, "'Believers' do not have the ability to help." Maria and Alexandrino share this opinion. They notice that Pentecostals take only a Bible when they visit hospitals and prisons.

Baruc and Edson say that "believers" are known as greedy. Edson, a believer, suffers from this criticism. A friend once told him, "After you became a 'believer' you became stingy." Edson explains that this friend is an alcoholic who had asked him for money. Edson refused and offered food instead because he knew his friend wanted money for drinking, and as a "believer" Edson could not give money for that. Baruc, whose parents are "believers," says that believers are considered tightwads because they value parsimony.

Although Pentecostals do not expect help from their churches, they do expect help from one another. Immediately after Neusa's husband died, she suffered a period of serious economic hardship. She was disappointed with most members of her church because no one helped her. Only a young believer from a church in another neighborhood gave her money to buy food. But she was not disappointed with the church as an institution. She did not expect the pastor to offer the church's money to help her. Similarly, Sebastião did not expect to receive economic support from his church when he was unemployed, explaining that the church did not have enough money for such aid. Sometimes the pastor gave him bus fare to return home, but never more than that.

Pentecostals I interviewed say that their church never uses money obtained through the tithe to help members with economic difficulties. Nevertheless, some Pentecostal churches pay the burial expenses of poor members and help unemployed believers (Novaes 1985; Page 1984). In this manner, churches offer a kind of social insurance for their members. A Brazil for Christ (*Brasil para Cristo*) pastor delivered a sermon that emphasized the individual duty of tithing, explaining that the church must help only those who have fulfilled this obligation. The aid is a kind of exchange. It does not release the poor from their economic responsibilities. Therefore, this practice cannot be identified as traditional charity.

An ordinary member of a Pentecostal church normally does not receive any material help from it. On the contrary, members tithe and give offerings to their churches, which they consider to be as poor as themselves. For this reason, these churches are perceived by outsiders as exploiters of the poor. For the majority of Pentecostal individuals and families, their churches do not offer any extra income as an institution. For some individuals, however, these churches become an alternative source of income, and sometimes the sole source.

The main leadership positions in the Assembly of God—pastors, *presbíteros* (presbyters), and *diáconos* (deacons)—are paid positions (Aubrée 1984). Victorino, one of my interviewees, is now a pastor. He used to be a mason but left his secular occupation after he became a pastor.

In this respect, Pentecostal churches are economically similar to the Afro-Spiritist centers in general, Umbanda as well as Candomblé. Both religious groups create new job opportunities and careers for some poor people. They offer economic survival and sometimes socioeconomic upward mobility for their leaders. There are many examples in Brazil of Afro-Brazilian Spiritist leaders who became well known and obtained large sums of money through their religious activities. Father Edu, a well-known Umbanda leader in Olinda, a city adjacent to Recife, is an example of a poor black male who failed in his attempts to become a priest. But as an Umbanda leader he obtained a great deal of money and fame by performing religious rituals and making "spiritual works" (*trabalhos feitos*) for a variety of individuals and organizations, including popular singers and soccer teams. He became famous after Náutico Club, one of the soccer teams for whom he worked, won a championship.

In contrast, to find a career opportunity in the Catholic and historical Protestant churches is more difficult for people from poor areas. The requirements of high education and celibacy make the career of a Catholic priest even less attainable for the Brazilian poor, as one pastoral agent told me in an interview. Recently, some Pentecostal churches have seemed to follow the pattern of historical Protestantism and have required more theological foundations for their pastors. Although the Assembly of God has two formal college-level seminaries in Brazil, both in the state of São Paulo, it still recruits most of its leadership from the poor. But, as the historical Protestant churches do, some Pentecostal churches recruit their leaders from a higher economic level than those of the leaders of the Assembly of God. In Alto José do Pinho, the pastors of both the Baptist and the Pentecostal Fousquare Gospel churches are from other social strata.

A career as a Pentecostal pastor provides many benefits. In addition to a salary, Pentecostal leaders have access to non-monetary advantages offered by the church. For example, pastors in the Assembly of God have their housing guaranteed by the church. Near most churches, the church provides a house where the pastor can live; if he prefers to live elsewhere, he can choose someone to be the caretaker (*zelador*) of the church and live there in the pastor's place. In Recife, where there are more churches than pastors, I observe that two church caretakers are children of presbyters. In the church I visited in Rio de Janeiro state, the pastor's daughter worked as the church's janitor and lived in the house near the church. In such cases, relatives of religious leaders also benefit materially from the leader's work at the church.

Religious careers in this church are not available to women, and although women may become strong leaders, they are never paid for their religious work. For instance, Neusa and Creuza are both important leaders in the Assembly of God; they converted their husbands, who subsequently entered upon religious careers that were not open to their wives. Women can benefit from the material support offered to leaders only indirectly, through their husbands' positions. Nevertheless, some official male leadership may be supported by the unofficial leadership of wives. Both Neusa and Creuza, as well as Roxinha, entered the Assembly of God before their husbands, and when their husbands converted, the women already were well known in the church. They pushed their husbands to study the Bible and occupy leadership positions that they, as women, could not obtain. Roxinha says her husband knows how to read and can go further than she can in Bible study.

Despite the fact that helping the needy is not an institutional concern of the Assembly of God, the example of homeless families living in halls beside churches illustrates how the church offers occasional aid to its members. Nevertheless, Pentecostals do not expect help from their churches. In this respect, their relationship to the church differs from the Brazilian cultural pattern of paternalist authority, which is present in relationships with the government and with employers. This cultural pattern is also present in family relationships and, traditionally, in the Catholic church.

CEBS AND MATERIAL SUPPORT

As mentioned earlier, the CEB attitude toward material support for the poor differs from that of Pentecostal churches. CEB people are very concerned with helping the poorest. Alice and Odete, leaders of CEBs, recall that the first activities of their groups involved collecting food from their neighbors to distribute to the neediest. The traditional practice of charity is very common among CEBs throughout Brazil (Castro 1987; Hewitt 1986, 1987; Petrini 1984).

Despite the fact that Alice's and Odete's CEBs have developed social assistance activities, these practices become less important when their groups begin to internalize the pastoral agents' message, or, in the language of CEB people, when they "move forward in the *caminhada*" (journey).

Alice described how her group's "journey" changed this practice. According to Alice, two things influenced her group to make changes: the limits to its social work—people who were helped never improved; and the reflections her group made about these activities during a training (*treinamento*) led by pastoral agents. The consciousness-raising process is a consequence of pastoral agents' work (Adriance 1986). That is, pastoral agents conduct the steps of people's consciousness raising. "Training days" are important parts of this work. Alice explained how her group changed its opinion about charity after a day of reflection with pastoral agents. She said, "In the assistance respect, we did a lot. [At that time] we used to have a *treinamento* every two months. The training used to be a day of studying. This study was for us to tell our experiences of what we had done . . . to exchange experiences. The result [of this study] was that we realized that it [assistance] was not the [right] way. Through the assistance we would never change anything. Assistance is this: You make and give to the other, then they do not participate in anything. They just receive, they thank you and it is finished. . . . Doing things for people does not help them improve, but doing things with people helps them improve."

This new vision on charity is shared by other CEB leaders. At a meeting of CEBs in Rio de Janeiro, one CEB member criticized another Catholic movement (the *Vicentinos*) because of its emphasis on traditional charity, or assistance. Another CEB member, Margarida, said that CEBs in her community try to help those who have economic problems, but she distinguished this practice from the traditional practice of charity. She compared the CEB vision of the church with the traditional vision held by other religious movements. She said, "I have a sister who participates a lot, but she does not have the same view of the church. She has a view of 'charity.' She participates in the Charismatic Movement. Her faith is of charity."

Although CEB leaders are known in the community as very charitable people, the practice of assistance is not an official part of the CEBs. They do offer economic help, but they prefer strategies that cannot be identified with traditional charity. First, they activate the informal network and organize people to help one another and to build streets, bridges, and houses, or to save money. Second, they obtain material facilities through

their political struggle. In both cases, these strategies benefit
the entire poor neighborhood. For instance, all residents of
the Alto do Carneiro neighborhood in Recife benefit from the
struggle for electric power. Similarly, the CEB demands enable
the entire population of Alto José do Pinho in Recife to profit
from the legalization of property ownership and from the area's
new public school. In addition, CEBs try to obtain support for
their sociopolitical activities from people who do not attend
their meetings.

The material aid obtained through political struggle tends to
benefit the community as a whole, rather than individual CEB
members. I did not discover any CEB members who had obtained personal benefits from a politician. In this respect, the
CEB attempts to break with assistance practices of traditional
Catholicism. CEBs try to transform people's goodwill toward
helping others into a political practice, and they also help isolated individuals solve their personal problems. Alice said her
CEB helped a woman who was ill and homeless. Members had
her admitted to a hospital, and when she was healthier, they
helped her build a house. Margarida recalled the aid offered by
her community to a poor man and his family. When the man
became ill, the community supported him and his family for
eight months until he recovered. Neither individuals helped
by Alice's and Margarida's CEBs were active members of these
religious groups, nor of the Catholic church. These people,
including those who lived in the chapel hall at Alto José do
Pinho, were the neighborhood's neediest, rather than members
or leaders of the group.

Religious affiliation is not a factor in determining who the
CEBs will help. Therefore, the majority of CEB leaders never
receive material aid, since most have been recruited among the
better-off in a neighborhood. This is true of Margarida. Even
when her husband was ill and she had little money, she never
received economic help from the community. She explained
that it was never necessary. Odete also noted that the active

CEB participants, in general, never need material help from
the group. Instead of receiving help from the group, many
CEB leaders actually spend their own money to help others.
Alice related how she saved money and gave it to others so that
they could install electricity in their homes. Lúcio said he and
another leader of his group once gave money to help pay the
priest's salary. Margarida's husband used to lend money to his
fellow workers.

The paid leadership in the Catholic church includes priests,
nuns, and seminarians. Usually these people are from outside
the community, and to obtain these paid positions the individuals must leave their original communities and submit to a
long preparation. Therefore, when someone from a poor community becomes a priest or a nun, he or she expresses a worldview that is different from that held by other members of his
or her community. Odete, from Alto José do Pinho, recalled
how twelve girls from this Recife neighborhood had wished
to become nuns, but after spending six months in a convent,
all twelve changed their minds. Odete's sister had also wanted
to be a nun, but despite being an active Catholic, Odete was
not pleased with her sister's idea. A seminarian, one of the pastoral agents in Alto do Carneiro, also tried to dissuade a young
female leader from becoming a nun. The seminarian believed
that if this young woman went to live in a convent, she would
suffer a difficult adaptation process and her CEB would miss
her presence.

A religious career in the Catholic church requires one to
adopt a lifestyle that is very different from that of most church
members. The lifestyle of official leaders (priests and nuns) in
the Catholic church tends to be more restrictive than that of
a Pentecostal leader, especially because of the celibacy requirement. This restrictiveness makes the career less attractive to
young people and widens the gap between religious leaders
and the general population. Additionally, because of the outside leadership of pastoral agents, local CEB leaders do not at-

tain the same degrees of power and autonomy in their religious groups as Pentecostals and Afro-Spiritist leaders do in theirs.

AFRO-BRAZILIAN SPIRITISM AND MATERIAL SURVIVAL

Kardecist Spiritist centers place a high value on social work. As they do all over the country, they offer in Recife shelters for elderly people and schools for poor children, among other services. Several interviewees mentioned help from Kardecist Spiritists. For instance, when they were children, Maria and Maria José (from Alto José do Pinho) studied in a school supported by Kardecist Spiritists. Kardecist Spiritists also organize the Kilo Campaign in order to obtain food or money for the very poorest. Ilze also benefited from Spiritist charity. When she was pregnant, she received a package of baby clothes from a Spiritist group in Rio de Janeiro. Ilze's sister, a Spiritist, helped her obtain the gift.

Most of these Kardecist organizations for charity are organized by people from a higher social level than that of the population studied. Maria José said that before she became a believer, she had been very impressed by how polite and educated the Spiritist people were in the school where she studied. Kardecist Spiritism is a middle-class religion and has some social prestige (Aguiar 1978; Brown 1986). Almost all my interviewees who practiced any kind of Afro-Brazilian religion preferred to identify themselves only as Spiritists, a generic term for both Kardecist and Afro-Brazilian Spiritism. This explains why in surveys on religious preferences in Brazil, Spiritists make up a higher proportion than do Afro-Brazilian religion practitioners. Kardecist Spiritists, however, do not like to be identified with the Afro-Brazilian Spiritists and often stress their differences.

Umbanda practitioners adopt the Kardecist attitude toward charity. Graças expressed her concern over the issue of aiding other people. José affirmed that "we cannot refuse people who ask for help." And Luís's dream is to open a school for poor children at his center. But none of the religious groups to which these people belong has any organized charity work. The leader of the group may help someone in need by using his own resources, as Graças recounted, or with the aid of another person from the center, as José described in his interview.

Umbanda's help is individual, and its conception of charity includes spiritual aid (Brown 1986), but richer Umbanda groups in different parts of Brazil do offer institutional aid services. But the institutional aid described by Brown and the aid offered by Spiritists in Recife function merely on the level of personal assistance. Traditional Afro-Brazilian religious groups, such as Candomblé and Xangô, do not offer institutional economic help and are not concerned with charity.

The Afro-Brazilian religious groups help the poor to survive by offering jobs for their leaders. As with Pentecostals, religious jobs and careers in these religious groups constitute the most instrumental aspect in the material survival of the poor. Many "fathers and mothers of saints" (religious leaders of those groups) are able to survive because of the religious work they perform. Some leaders engage in these activities as an additional source of income, although the income does not serve as the motivating factor. Others occasionally perform religious jobs and are paid for them, although they are not leaders of any religious "center." This is the case of Graças and Luís, who receive money by performing a fortune-telling ritual known as *jogar búzios* (reading shells).[1] These people also receive money from upper-class clients (Brown 1986). In this respect, Afro-Spiritist groups differ from Pentecostal churches, whose members have more homogeneous social origins.

In contrast to the other religious groups analyzed, religious careers in Afro-Spiritism and Kardecist Spiritism do not differ between men and women, with both sexes having equal opportunities. In addition, little intellectual preparation is required of the leaders, a fact that provides equal leadership opportunities for people of different social levels.

RELIGION AND THE NETWORK
OF MUTUAL SUPPORT

The network of mutual support is an important instrument in helping to alleviate some of the struggles of the poor. The roles of kinship and neighborhood networks as strategies for helping the poor survive have been described in great detail in anthropological literature.[2] The life histories analyzed show that religious groups establish networks of exchange that also help the poor survive. Pentecostalism creates an alternative network of support (Page 1984). For most Pentecostals, this informal network is more helpful for their material survival than the institutional church itself. Many of the Pentecostals interviewed told of fellow believers who helped them find jobs, gave or lent them money, or offered some other form of support. Neusa's first job was found by a "sister in the faith," the term Pentecostals normally use to address one another. Neusa's daughter's job and Sebastião's first job in Recife were also found by members of their churches. Eurídice said that someone from the church used to pay for her education when she was a child. As an adult, Eurídice chose a young fellow believer to be her children's baby-sitter in exchange for free housing, board, and a small salary. Creuza, who works as a dressmaker, said that almost all her clients were from her church. Creuza also told how she helps church members build their houses. The literature about Pentecostals is filled with many similar examples.[3]

The function of creating an alternative network of mutual help is not exclusive to Pentecostalism. As mentioned earlier, this practice is part of the lifestyle of Brazilian poor people (Leeds and Leeds 1970) and is not an innovation of any single religious group. Umbanda's "father of saint" might use his many connections to help members of his center. The behavior of José, a "father of saint," or "caretaker of saint" (*zelador de santo*), as he prefers to call himself, illustrates Diana Brown's observations. José is always ready to activate his network to find a job or medical care for anyone who needs help, regardless of whether the person is a member of José's center. José related how he once was able to obtain a bed for a needy person in a crowded hospital by using his influence with a male nurse in this hospital who was also his "son in the saint." Although José practices a kind of Candomblé, he holds a Umbanda values and emphasizes the importance of helping others. Candomblé and Umbanda connect people from different geographical neighborhoods and social classes (Brown 1986), and this mixture offers a large network with exchanges among classes, or vertical connections.

Historical Protestant churches also use vertical networks for material aid. But these churches have relatively few members among the poor and are composed mainly of middle-class people. For instance, in Alto José do Pinho, some Baptists say that their pastor has helped their sons to find jobs. The Baptist pastor of Alto José do Pinho described the importance of the pastor's role in helping the people of his church to be employed, stressing that the pastor's survival depends on the members. Another example is a young Presbyterian who has also received strong support from her pastor, who helped her to find a job and housing. Both Baptist and Presbyterian pastors were from the middle class.

In contrast to the historical Protestant groups, CEBs and Pentecostal churches have almost no adherents from the middle class, but CEBs link their leaders with people from higher classes through pastoral agents and other religious groups of the Catholic church. Pentecostalism now has some adherents from the middle class, but they are still few, at least in the Assembly of God church. Pentecostalism, however, creates a network among different geographical areas. For example, the Assembly of God widens its network by involving people from different geographical areas, rather than people of different classes. Many Pentecostals from Alto José do Pinho speak of activities they have attended in other neighborhoods and mention friends from other areas whom they have met through the church.

Despite connecting their leaders with people from other classes and neighborhoods, the CEBs do not create an active network of support with people from outside their neighborhood boundaries. Even within the community, CEBs do not create new connections among people, but simply reinforce those that already exist. CEBs try to activate the neighbors' network of mutual support and direct them toward collective goals, rather than foster individual support. For instance, before Alice became a CEB member, her house had been built by her brother-in-law's friends. These people organized themselves into a group for mutual help, which they called *mutirão*, in order to build houses for one another. Later, Alice's CEB proposed the organization of *mutirões* to build a bridge in the area. Margarida's CEB used the same process to restore an old chapel and construct a community house.

The CEB emphasis on the collective use of neighborhood networks and on aiding the neediest decreases the economic advantages of being a CEB leader. After the opening of a new school that his CEB had struggled for, both Lúcio (a CEB leader) and a Pentecostal obtained a job there. Similarly, the houses built by CEBs may be inhabited not only by CEB leaders but also by non-CEB members, as happened in Alto José do Pinho.

RELIGIOUS AFFILIATION AND
PREVIOUS SUPPORT NETWORKS

Pentecostals maintain most of the relationships with kin and neighbors that they had before conversion (Novaes 1985; Page 1984). That is, they adopt new networks without substituting old ones. In poor areas, the network of relatives, especially the closest (parents, children, and siblings), seems to be the most important source of support. Interviewees from all religious groups referred to the help they received from, or offered to, their relatives. Lúcio was helped by his cousin and, later, by his father-in-law. Maria, a Spiritist and *Umbandista*, called her eldest daughter her main economic supporter. Eurídice, a Pentecostal, lends her house to her parents when they do not have enough money to pay rent. Manoel, also Pentecostal, received economic help from his daughter, a Baptist.

A popular strategy to solve housing problems is the establishment of large households with many people from the same family (Clark 1988). Margarida, a CEB leader who lives with her husband and children, has also shared her home with her two brothers, who helped her when her husband was seriously ill. Socorro is a CEB member and her sister is a Pentecostal; however, when her sister became pregnant, she went to live with Socorro's family. Among *Umbandistas* and Spiritists there is the example of Maria's household. Because of a lack of housing, Maria's third daughter, married and with a family of her own, was forced to live with her mother, brothers, and sisters.

Poor households are frequently very large. João, an Afro-Spiritist from Alto José do Pinho, and Sebastião, a Pentecostal from Alto do Carneiro, cannot tell how many people live in their houses until they stop to think and count. Eleven people live in Sebastião's house: he and his wife, his five children, his two grandchildren, his wife's grandchild, and his mother-in-law. For most of my interviewees, the obligation toward family members is stronger than the commitment to a religious movement. Benedita, a CEB leader, has been busy taking care of her grandchildren, although she would prefer not to be raising children at this point in her life. Instead, she would like to participate in meetings and community work, but she cannot abandon her daughter, who needs to work and does not have anyone else to care for her children. Benedita tried to become a believer (or Pentecostal) like her husband, Sebastião. She explained, "I think it is correct for a family to be unified, at least in its religion. But sometimes this is not possible. You know, each person has a way of being, of thinking. He [Sebastião] thinks in one way, and I think in another."

Other people experience family conflict because of their religion. Wives in particular suffer opposition from their husbands because of their religious commitments. Neusa, for example, had several problems with her husband before he converted. He did not want Neusa to participate in the Assembly of God. Margarida's sister-in-law, who also belongs to the Assembly of God, faced problems with her husband because of her new religion. Odete's husband used to prohibit her from going to CEB meetings. Alice is a widow, but has had similar problems with her mother, who does not like her to go to CEB night meetings alone. Both Alice and Odete have been successful in convincing their mother and husband, respectively, to join them at the CEBs. In order to reconcile family and religion, people often try to convert their close relatives.

When women convert to Pentecostalism, family conflict generally seems to decrease (Page 1984). In contrast, some domestic conflicts emerge with the engagement of the women in CEBs (Petrini 1984). This difference may reflect the different roles prescribed for women by CEBs and Pentecostalism; however, it is not yet clear whether Pentecostalism reinforces family ties more than CEBs. The family network did not have religious frontiers, and there was great religious diversity among extended family members and even within the nuclear family. In Morro da Conceição, another poor neighborhood in Recife, I found that most Pentecostals (70 percent) and Afro-Brazilian Spiritists (100 percent) live with relatives who practice other religions (Mariz 1992). Examples of that diversity include Socorro, who participates in a CEB and has sisters who are Pentecostals from the Assembly of God, and Edmar, a Pentecostal who lives with her mother, who is a Baptist, and with her father, a Spiritist. After many years as an *Umbandista*, Agnaldo's mother has recently become a Pentecostal, but Agnaldo remains an *Umbandista*. A similar case exists in the family of Conceição and Graças; although their mother had been a Baptist, these two sisters are *Umbandistas*. Zefinha has an Adventist son and a Spiritist daughter, and she attends both Catholic and Protestant churches because she believes that both are equally good. Maria Omar, an active Catholic from a CEB, has a son who is married to a "believer." Manoel is Pentecostal, but his wife and daughter are Baptists. Judite is Baptist, but her sister is Spiritist; José, the leader ("father of saint") in Afro-Brazilian Spiritism mentioned earlier, has a Pentecostal sister. Both Judite and José say they never talk about religion with their sisters, so as to avoid arguments. In fact, people often avoided discussing religion with their relatives in order to maintain family relationships. In my research, it was difficult to find a religiously homogeneous Pentecostal household. Marion Aubrée (1984) also observed many Pentecostals who did not share their beliefs with spouses or children.

Another kind of support network occurs between housekeepers and their *patroas*, or the ladies of the house. Pentecostals such as Roxinha, Neusa, and Anésio receive help from their employers' families, as do Faustina, a traditional Catholic, and Socorrinho, an Afro-Spiritist. Fewer people from CEBs mention help given by their employers, which could be explained by the low number of maids who participate in CEBs. Among my interviewees, Socorro, the sole CEB member who works as a housekeeper, did in fact mention that she received material support from her employer's family.

DISADVANTAGES OF THE
SUPPORT NETWORK

Participation in a horizontal network, such as kinship, may help some to endure poverty, but may also hinder others from overcoming poverty (Stack 1974). Actually, people with a better economic situation may lose money when they participate in horizontal social networks of mutual support. For example, Maria Omar and Ilze say it is difficult to sell goods in their own neighborhoods because neighbors ask to buy on credit (*comprar fiado*), and some of them never pay later. Maria do Carmo says her father lost his little shop because his clients, to whom he sold on credit, never paid him. Margarida's husband had a bad experience lending money to some friends, who never repaid him. Socorrinho acknowledges that she put some of her own money into the neighborhood association when she was its president. Alice has spent her savings to help people install electricity in their houses. Luís says that he lost money from his small business when he allowed his brother-in-law to run it.

It is difficult to tell if people's economic situation would have been better if they had not offered this assistance. Despite the fact that some people lost money because of their support network, other people were able to participate in this network and improve their own—and someone else's—economic condition. This is the case of a supermarket owner in Alto José do Pinho, who, according to Maria, has helped many people but still has managed to improve his own economic situation. Maria tells how, when her husband worked at a supermarket, the owner helped the couple buy their house and a truck. The supermarket owner bought the house and sold it to Maria and her husband on an installment plan. This case illustrates that participation in the horizontal network does not always hinder social improvement. Depending on the kind of help offered and to whom it is offered, this help can also be profitable. For instance, Aniceto helps many women find jobs as maids, and sometimes receives a "finder's fee" from the employer.

In summary, despite their different values and assumptions, most religious groups offer material aid to the poor and can be considered economically useful for poor people's survival. Nevertheless, each religious group offers different kinds of material aids and has different perceptions of this help. Some, such as the Spiritist (Afro-Brazilian and Kardecist), historical Protestant, and Catholic groups (especially the traditional) tend to offer assistance to the poor. These material aids are generally given occasionally, with the goal of helping only the poorest to overcome critical situations. In contrast, Pentecostalism does not stress these activities. Pentecostal groups, however, can be economically instrumental for their leaders, offering them income on a regular basis. Similarly, Afro-Brazilian Spiritism provides the poor with an alternative source of income. Both religious groups offer religious jobs for their leaders, and these leaders may be economically successful because of their religious positions. Pentecostalism and Afro-Spiritism tend to emphasize individual help; they differ from CEBs, which are more concerned with helping to improve the community. CEBs do not offer new careers and do not become a new source of income for individual leaders. In addition, they tend to deemphasize the assistance offered to individuals.

CHAPTER V

Political Strategies for Coping with Poverty

Residents' associations are the most important political instruments in poor urban Brazilian neighborhoods, and they represent the strongest social movement in Recife (Assies 1992). Although few people were actively participating in residents' associations in the poor areas I researched, many knew of the material benefits the associations brought to their neighborhoods, and they valued these organizations for those material gains. Although economic interests motivate most political struggles, this is particularly apparent among the poor, whose struggle for power expresses itself concretely in their everyday struggle for survival. While trying not to reduce political activities to economic or survival-oriented behaviors, I think it is important to acknowledge that the political involvement of poor people depends largely on their material needs and that politics offers material gains for groups and individuals.

Therefore, when religious groups act politically or try to transform the political behaviors of poor people, they may be helping the poor to solve immediate problems caused by poverty or to improve their situation through political means. While the relationship between religion and politics in Latin America has been largely analyzed in terms of the criticism each religion makes of the class structure and power distribution of the society,[1] it is also important to consider how poor individuals and communities obtain material improvements through politics. It is extremely important to stress the economic aspects of political behavior. Of course, material improvements can solve the problems of some poor individuals, but not poverty in general, for poverty has wider implications. Some political attitudes that are instrumental in individuals' survival may even hinder social change and a solution to poverty as a broad social problem. On the other hand, despite their long-term economic goals, political behaviors that attempt to change the class structure and power distribution may not produce immediate economic improvements. Nevertheless, the ability of political behaviors to bring immediate alleviation to the hardships of poverty is an important factor in explaining poor people's political values and attitudes.

POLITICS AMONG THE POOR

Poor people are relatively new political actors on the Brazilian stage. For more than a century after Brazil's independence in 1822, the country's political scene was dominated by rural elites who controlled the votes of rural citizens, who made up the majority of the population. Most poor people were neither organized nor engaged in any significant political movement, and because of their illiteracy, they were unable to vote. Electoral participation increased with the democratization of 1945, the development of industry, the growth of the urban population, and a decrease in the illiteracy rate. During that period, as Love (1970, 18) remarks, "the changing nature of rural politics brought into question the previously accepted proposition that the literacy requirement was necessarily a progressive measure." But even before the elimination of the literacy requirement, the electoral participation of low-income groups had increased, and new urban groups had threatened the power of the rural elite and the patriarchal system.

The undermining of the power of rural elites and the increase in the number of low-income voters did not change the "clientele" structure of the Brazilian state. Despite technological changes and the industrialization process that took place after the 1930s, the Brazilian state continued to "operate through informal networks and asymmetrical personal relationships" so that "political parties tended to represent local interests of political clients rather than national ideology" (Brown 1986). In other words, this period saw the emergence of populist politics in Brazil. The increasing electoral participation of the poor did not initially result in political changes because their participation resulted only from an extension of the patronage system.

Because of the state's clientele structure, politics in Brazil tends to unite the rich and poor in a sort of "protector–protected" relationship. In fact, most Brazilians perceive politics as a way to exchange votes for jobs, favors, or protection. The poor, in particular, have a very material conception of politics. An election is regarded as a bargaining period (Hoffnagel 1978; Novaes 1985; Stoll 1984; and others). The poor know that rich people need their votes, and they try to use this power for material advantages. Therefore, through politics, poor people establish networks of exchange with rich people. The poor receive economic aid and give political legitimization. These exchanges occur both on an individual basis between politicians and a single poor person and on a large scale between politicians and associations of the poor, such as Carnival clubs or religious groups. Thus these groups operate as interest groups for the poor.

Actually, "patronage ties" have been an important strategy for survival and economic mobility in Brazil for different social classes (Leeds 1964). With the coming of industrialization, few workplaces offered opportunities to develop such a relationship between boss and workers. This kind of relationship is still common only among people who work as housekeepers, no matter which religion they practice. Neusa, a black Pentecostal, says the family for whom she has worked since her husband died has helped her. Anesio, a retired factory worker and a Pentecostal, explains that his wife works as a maid for a middle-class family and says his grandson is protected by this family. Henrique, a traditional Catholic with no religious involvement says he began working as a domestic servant in a wealthy household and through this family obtained a public-sector job. Socorro, one of the few maids I studied who participates in a CEB, says she is helped by the family for whom she works.

Since industrialization began, politicians have attempted to perform the role of protective boss for the urban masses. Politicians were perceived as people from higher social classes who could protect the poor. The exchanges of material gains for political power were prevalent in both poor neighborhoods I researched in the northeastern city of Recife: Alto José do Pinho and Alto do Carneiro. The Alto José do Pinho neighborhood was protected by a family of politicians, the Correias. The strongest leader of this family was described by an interviewee as "the God on Earth in the 'Alto.'" He was considered a good politician because he helped many individuals cope with their personal difficulties and because he brought public services to the area. Good politicians were those who gave jobs to their constituents and brought improvements to the neighborhood. Some inhabitants of Alto José do Pinho refer to the good politicians of the past as those who helped them, or someone they know, to find a job. In fact, the elderly from Alto José do Pinho recall the populist period as the "time of the politicians," explaining that politicians brought many material improvements to the area, including health assistance, paved roads, and electric power. One interviewee said, "Before the politicians, this hill was very 'backward'."

The formation of the Alto do Carneiro neighborhood also illustrates the political patronage relationship. In the late 1950s and early 1960s, Newton Carneiro, a wealthy politician, gave all the land of this area to the people living there in exchange for their votes. In return, the neighborhood was named for its political patron. But Carneiro has lost elections and political influence. Likewise, the Correia family has lost its influence in Alto José do Pinho. These changes reflect important transformations in Brazilian society and politics. First, the expansion and the social differentiation of lower sectors made it impossible to develop a geographically based patronage. Second, the failure of the "populist" experiment[2] fostered transformations in the nature of the Brazilian state and the emergence of a new political element among poor people: social movements.

Because of social differentiation among the poor, patronage ties are now established mainly on the basis of poor people's associations, not on geographical distinctions. Thus, most of poor people's religious or leisure groups have been engaged in this kind of political activity. This fact may be perceived by someone who visits the area. Many Carnival clubs, Afro-Brazilian Spiritist centers, and other association meeting places have signs on them bearing the name of a politician or political party.

Although some social movements, such as residents' associations (*Associações de Moradores*) have existed since the 1930s and 1940s, their boom years have been much more recent, reflecting transformations in the nature of the state.[3] The contradictions between the legitimizing social policies of the state and their obvious inefficiencys in offering public services have fostered the emergence of social movements (Cardoso 1983). Nevertheless, the state may also create social movements directly, as occurred in Recife.

Neighborhood associations emerged in Recife in the 1950s and were organized by leftist parties that had succeeded in electing a mayor (Cézar 1985). This candidate, with the help of the Communist party, organized residents' associations to expand his base of support and allow the direct participation of the lower sectors in his administration. Through these associations, he also intended to break clientele ties. Recife's city government helped create the city's first residents' associations. Therefore the associations addressed their requests to the state, but were not opposed to it (Cézar 1985). A similar process of creating residents' associations by the state also occurred in Recife under a nonleftist mayor in the 1980s. Almost 50 percent of all residents' associations in Recife were founded between 1978 and 1982. The Recife City Hall directly promoted the creation of some of these associations in order to increase the penetration of the ruling party in areas controlled by opposing parties (Moura 1988, 16).

Although the presence of residents' associations is directly related to the hardships of poverty, these movements are not spontaneous (Jacobi 1987). They emerge through the action of external agents with definite political interests (Cézar 1985). These external agents may try to maintain the same political structure and establish new patronage ties, or they may aim to change the power structure and political style. In the early 1980s in Recife, City Hall and the Catholic church were the two major external agents that fostered the growth of residents' associations (Moura 1988). Both agents played an important role in the residents' association of Alto José do Pinho.

Although some residents' associations and social movements can be used to reestablish patronage ties, in general they become a new means of political participation for the poor. Through these movements, political action expands beyond

elections and takes on a larger dimension. Though the performance of residents' associations varies among communities, the
organizations generally have become very important for Brazil's
poor people. Therefore, to understand the political attitudes of
each religious group, it is important to understand the relationships formed between the different religious groups and the
residents' associations.

BRAZILIAN AFRO-SPIRITISTS
AND POLITICS

The worldview of Afro-Brazilian Spiritism in general, and Umbanda in particular, reproduces the social relationship of patronage within Brazilian society as a whole (Brown 1986). This
relationship is also found in traditional folk Catholicism. In
these religions, people exchange vows, or obligations (*obriga-
ções*), or promises (*promessas*) with their saints and *orixás*[4] in
order to obtain favors or protection. Likewise, they expect jobs
and favors from politicians in exchange for their votes and loy-
alty.

Luís, a slim, black Afro-Spiritist from Alto José do Pinho,
illustrates this relationship. He claims that he gave up voting
because politicians did not find him a job. As the owner of an
Afro-Spiritist center, he supports a city councilman who prom-
ised to help him open a small school in his center, but never
did so. Pinça, the owner of another Afro-Spiritist center in Alto
José do Pinho, also expresses disappointment with the politicians she supported because they did not help her with her
religious center. These two individuals reflect a widespread disappointment in the neighborhood, where most people feel that
politicians have not honored their promises. Nevertheless, the
poor maintain that they need to know politicians in order to
help them obtain jobs. Yet very few people, such as Maria's
daughter, actually got a job from a politician.

Different religious affiliations do not present any clear shift in expectations. The legitimacy of this kind of exchange was not questioned by people who joined different religious groups, even those who joined CEBs. I have observed a different attitude in this respect only among some CEB leaders. For instance, a member of a CEB from Alto José do Pinho criticized a certain politician who did not give "at least a job" to the leader of her CEB, who had worked very hard in the politician's campaign. This leader, however, was disappointed with the politician, not because of the job, but because he did not listen to the community's demands. Another member of a CEB told how she earned money working in a political campaign. She did not hide the fact that, for her, this political work was as much of a job as any other.

Only one of the Afro-Spiritists interviewed, Socorrinho, is actively engaged in a residents' association. Although she accepts the major assumptions of Umbanda described by Diana Brown (1986), Socorrinho interprets these assumptions in a way that helps her find religious meaning in her political activities.

Afro-Brazilian Spiritism does not become involved in collective action. In general, individualist assumptions and the concept of Karma, which is clearly stated by Umbanda and accepted in different degrees by Candomblé followers, tend not to ascribe religious meaning to political actions. I found no examples of an Afro-Brazilian Spiritist group striving for material improvement through social movements. As mentioned earlier, the political involvement of these groups follows the patronage style. The adoption of these religions, however, does not hinder individuals from engaging in social movements or similar political activities. It is difficult to estimate how many members of this kind of religion also participate in social movements. Because of the persecution they suffered, and the prejudice they still experience,[5] Afro-Spiritists try to be discreet about their religious preference and avoid religious identification. Socorrinho described her surprise when she discovered that Chico, a fellow leader of a neighboring residents' association, is also an *Umbandista*. She did not expect this because, as a president of a neighborhood association, Chico has been involved with the Catholic church through the "shantytown pastoral" (*Pastoral da favela*).

These examples indicate that the Afro-Brazilian worldview is not an obstacle to political engagement. The flexibility and multiplicity of rules of this religion allow various attitudes toward politics. Socorrinho, for instance, perceives her political work as a personal spiritual calling that is part of her spiritual development. That is, her political work is simply a continuation of her spiritual work. It is important to note, however, that she considers this calling to be very personal. Socorrinho does not believe that politics has to play a part in everyone's religious concerns, nor does she think that everyone must be politically active. As we discuss later in the chapter, this view differs greatly from that of CEB members.

The literature on Afro-Brazilian Spiritism has stressed, in general, its political conservatism and uncritical view. Nevertheless, some authors have suggested that these groups may have a critical view and that it may be separate from patronage ties. There may be potentially political groups that would be able to support lower-sector interests (Ireland 1988). Such groups could be useful instruments for political participation. This view tends to see these groups as democratic because of their members' economic homogeneity. But economic homogeneity is not a sufficient condition to make a group autonomous and representative of its members' interests. In order to attain such representativeness and autonomy, these groups would need to have an internal democratic structure. This structure could allow more participation of the members and could help people develop a different relationship with the authorities and the state. Following the same argument, Carnival clubs are not democratic groups; their political internal structure is highly authoritarian and does not allow equal participation for members.[6]

Some of the social movements among the poor face internal problems with political participation. Leaders from low-income sectors frequently adopt the authoritarian style and behavior of their richer patrons. For example, Ester, a Catholic woman from a *favela* in Rio de Janeiro who was striving to obtain land to build her house, criticized the leader of her *favela*'s residents' association because he was trying to obtain personal benefits from his position. A pastoral agent had a similar complaint about a rural union leader, claiming that he used his union power to obtain personal benefits for himself and his friends. The break with political clientelism and individuals' abuse of political power seems to depend on the development of a grassroots organization with an egalitarian internal structure, as well as a change in the political culture.

PENTECOSTALISM AND POLITICS

Pentecostal leaders have been shown to engage in politics despite their claim that they do not get involved in political activities. In addition, Pentecostals adopt clientele behaviors in the political sphere. For example, pastors frequently obtain paved streets or electrification of their churches through favors from politicians they have supported.[7]

More recently, Pentecostal churches have become more openly involved in politics, as have other Protestant churches. Brazil's National Congress includes a group of Protestant politicians with a political platform aimed at defending the interests of their churches.[8] Their religious identity is an important factor in their election campaigns, and Protestant churches have become political interest groups (Stoll 1986). A Pentecostal pastor I interviewed mentioned the importance of electing an *Evan-*

gélico (the term he used to refer to any Protestant person). He referred to some personal help he had obtained, stressing that such help was not illegal; in his view, in order to obtain his legal rights, he had to have the support of someone in the government. In contrast, ordinary Pentecostals do not mention any problem that has been solved with the help of politicians. This suggests that patronage ties may be useful for leaders of the churches or for the institutions themselves, but not for common members.

Despite the much-discussed authoritarianism of their doctrines,[9] some Pentecostals seem to have developed independent political and moral behaviors. In general, Pentecostal church members follow their pastors' electoral advice. Nevertheless, the individualism and apolitical values of Pentecostalism allow Pentecostals to reject their pastors' political instructions. I met Pentecostals who declared that they did not vote for the candidate supported by their church. Francisco Gomes's (1985) data indicate that this situation may occur frequently. Pentecostalism's emphasis on the individual's ability to know the truth through the Bible may allow for the development of independent political behavior.

Pentecostals do, however, display behaviors and statements that reveal individual independence on moral issues. Creuza and Sebastião are examples of this phenomenon. Creuza, a Pentecostal woman from Rio de Janeiro, criticizes the superficial, vain lifestyles of young believers. When someone argues that their pastor supports them, Creuza answers that she does not need a pastor to know what is right and wrong. Sebastião, a Pentecostal, feels free to disagree with some of the rules of his church. For instance, he drinks a little alcohol, which he does not consider sinful. He says that a little alcohol is good for one's health and that Jesus and the apostles also drank.

For Maria José, a former *Umbandista* who became a Pentecostal, the main difference between these two religions is the source of the Truth. She says she did not understand the basis on which the Umbandist and Spiritist rules and truths were defined. But in her new faith she can check the Bible for herself and discover what is right and wrong. Therefore, Pentecostals do not depend on their leaders, who are considered to be ordinary people like themselves, to learn what is right or wrong because they can consult "the Word of God" in the Bible. In their religion, the source of the Truth is independent of any one individual.

Pentecostals' low interest in joining social movements may be another consequence of Pentecostal individualist assumptions. Pentecostalism does not motivate individuals to participate in collective action, although some Pentecostals do join social movements and residents' associations. Abumanssur (1987) described an interesting case of a Pentecostal pastor who was an active leader in this kind of association in Rio de Janeiro. Another example of a Pentecostal who holds a political view independent from the one dominant in her church (the Assembly of God) is the federal deputy Benedita da Silva, who joined the most leftist party in Brazil, the Workers' party (*Partido dos Trabalhadores*, or PT). In November 1992, Benedita da Silva ran for mayor of Rio de Janeiro but was defeated in a hotly contested race.

Generally, Pentecostals show little interest in any social movement. They seem to become interested in these movements only when they perceive a chance of individual advantage. I met a Pentecostal woman, for instance, who was disappointed because she had not received a job from the mayor despite all her work in the residents' association's struggle for water. Another Pentecostal complained about the inefficiency of his neighborhood association in solving the problems on his street. Odete, a leader of the Alto José do Pinho residents' association and a CEB leader, observed that the "believers" supported the demand for a school in the area organized by the residents' association only after they realized that the school would bring jobs to the area. Thus, it seems that when Pentecostals have personal needs, they do participate in these kinds of political activities.

Pentecostals sometimes mistrust residents' associations because they are led by Catholics. Nevertheless, they seem aware of the possibilities inherent in these movements for the improvement of people's life conditions. This mixture of hesitation and the desire to participate in these associations is clear in the example of a believer who got up a petition (*abaixo-assinado*) that demanded improvements on his street and sent it to the Alto José do Pinho residents' association. He expected the association to send the petition to public officials, but he did not have the courage to attend association meetings himself.

For most Pentecostals, politics does not play an important role in their survival struggle, nor do ordinary members normally benefit from the patronage alliances of their leaders. Although their religion does not encourage them to join social movements, it does not prevent them from joining them. The expansion of these movements and their relative success in obtaining material benefits for the poor have attracted some Pentecostals. In the future, Pentecostals may become more involved in such movements. This is highly probable if the trend toward obtaining official recognition and power continues, and the declining presence of the Catholic church is not reversed. Pentecostalism as a doctrine is not opposed to this new style of political participation. Despite its conservatism and authoritarianism, Pentecostalism offers cognitive assumptions and values that may provide a base for a renewal in the political culture of the poor.

CEBS AND POLITICS

In contrast to the other groups analyzed, CEBs have a political as well as a religious origin. They began to emerge in the 1970s when concerns about social injustice and poverty led to a political renewal in some sectors of the Catholic church, particularly in Latin America. These sectors of the church named their political engagement an "option for the poor," indicating an assumption that poverty is a political problem.

Since the late 1970s, CEBs have captured the attention of social scientists and public opinion in general because of their political goals and activities. Most of the research on CEBs has attempted to assess their political consequences.[10] These studies have examined CEBs as part of the political evolution of the so-called progressive sector of the Catholic church.

In fact, poverty is the mobilizing factor, not only at the intellectual level of the political ideology of progressive Catholicism, but also for the everyday praxis of CEB members. Political activities of CEBs grow directly out of the situation of deprivation. This seems to be true also in the politicization of poor people generally, as was mentioned earlier.

The first step in CEB grassroots mobilization is a description of everyday needs and hardships. But deprivation without a political orientation does not create political motivation. Alice, a teacher, and Margarida, a housewife, are both widows and CEB leaders. Both women became concerned with the need to organize poor people in order to obtain their rights as well as social improvements. Both had seen injustices before coming to the group, but only after reflecting on these injustices in the CEBs did they perceive them as a political problem.

Considering CEB political activities as an instrument for coping with poverty may sound, to the progressive sectors of the Catholic church who have fostered it, like a misinterpretation of CEB political goals. Only those who are successful in surviving poverty are able to escape from it. Therefore, actions for survival are not necessarily opposed to social transformations.

CEBs are important political instruments in the Catholic church (Mainwaring 1986). Nevertheless, the church has other channels for political participation. In addition to CEBs, the Catholic church acts politically through declarations by the church hierarchy and through specific pastoral activities, named *Pastorais* (e.g., *Pastoral da favela*, to help people from the slums, and *Pastoral da terra*, to support the fight for land) which assist social movements in different ways, such as offering advice to leaders, especially in relation to legal questions, and providing lawyers' services and rooms for meetings. While *Pastorais* offer the technical assistance and support needed by social movements, CEBs mobilize and motivate the poor to organize themselves and to participate in these movements. CEBs cannot offer technical or material help to people, but only ideological support. They aim to develop a basic and long-term political work by getting people interested enough in politics to adopt a new political style of participation. In this respect, the activities of *Pastorais* are complementary to CEBs, and in general they work together. But in some areas CEBs are stronger than *Pastorais* while in other areas the situation is the opposite. For example, in the Recife neighborhood of Alto José do Pinho, there is no Pastoral performing an important role; but in the *favelas* of Rio de Janeiro city, there are *Pastorais* but no CEBs. Finally, in Duque de Caxias, a rural zone of greater Rio de Janeiro, CEBs work together with the *Pastoral da terra*. *Pastorais'* political works seem to be more strongly developed in areas of social conflict. Socorrinho, who is from Rio de Janeiro, looks to the *Pastoral da favela* when she needs to know how to deal with the bureaucratic state system in order to solve the water supply problem in her community. As an *Umbandista*, Socorrinho was not motivated by any Catholic religious groups to engage in a residents' association. Her political motivation was independent of the Catholic religion. She became involved in the Catholic *Pastoral da favela* because she was president of her community residents' association. In contrast, Margarida's initial motivation to participate in CEBs was purely religious. Later, this participation motivated her to engage in the *Pastoral da terra* and in politics.

Most of the CEB leaders I interviewed had experiences similar to Margarida's. They became leaders of residents' associations and involved in social movements as a consequence of their participation in CEBs. In all the areas I visited, CEBs had a very close relationship with residents' associations. Maria Omar in Alto José do Pinho stressed that all people's attempts at organization in this area have been motivated and supported by the Catholic church. Most of the leaders of CEBs in this area, including Lúcio, Odete, and Ernestina, are also directors of the residents' association. The same occurred in Alto dos Carneiros. In both neighborhoods, these leaders seemed less dedicated to CEBs than to residents' associations.

The CEBs, however, do provide important mobilizing power. In this respect, they offer a psychological strategy for coping with poverty by mobilizing people to organize themselves in order to improve their lives. Nevertheless, this religious mobilizing power does not reach many people. Only a few CEB members have developed a social and political concern (Macedo 1986). They are a small minority within the Catholic church. In Alto José do Pinho, home to approximately eight thousand people, there are, at most, twenty people who attend CEB meetings, and only about five of them are politically concerned leaders. As a pastoral agent acknowledged, politically aware leaders are as scarce "as yeast in dough." They are not quantitatively important. The importance of CEBs is not because of the number of people they politicize, but the creation of a leadership with a new political attitude. This helps explain why in 1982, people from CEB areas did not vote in opposition to the government, as pastoral agents and leaders would have expected (Betto 1984). Nevertheless, political behavior cannot merely be identified with electoral behavior (Adriance 1986) but must also include engagement in social movements. And CEBs seem to be successful in supporting social movements.

In addition to their role as a mobilizing factor, CEBs have a role in fostering a new political culture (Viola and Mainwaring 1987). CEBs try to avoid political clientelism, authoritarianism, and paternalistic leadership. As discussed in Chapter 3, there are limits to introducing the CEB's new political culture and behavior. Nevertheless, some new political values may be observed in CEB leaders' interviews. Alice described her shift from a perception of religion as offering a paternalistic charity to that of religion as defending a social organization of the poor in their struggle for survival. Margarida explained that, through CEBs, she and her husband discovered the power and the strength of the group. Before becoming CEB members, they used to make demands, as individuals, for community improvements. After their religious engagement, they decided to work with the group to create change. Other leaders, such as Odete, Ernestina, and Lucio, became involved in politics through CEBs, although their interviews gave no explicit indications of change. Ernestina explained that the creation of the residents' association in Alto José do Pinho allowed the CEBs of the area to be less politically active and made evangelization their primary concern.

An important political innovation of the CEBs is the presence of female leaders. CEBs politicize women by transforming everyday survival problems into a political problem. In the CEBs I visited, most members were women (about 70 to 80 percent). The same situation has been observed by researchers in different areas of Brazil and Latin America.[11] Through CEBs, many women enter the public sphere. While Pentecostalism strongly encourages men to be present in the private life of the family, CEBs encourage women to participate in the public world of politics. Female leadership, however, was not an innovation intentionally created by the CEBs, but a consequence of the absence of men in these groups. As Castro (1987) observed, and I noticed as well, the few men who participate in CEBs are more likely than women to obtain positions of leadership. This explains why there are always more men than women at CEB national meetings.

My data do not offer enough indications to determine whether CEBs were responsible for the development of social movements or only for the mobilization of leaders. In Alto José do Pinho, it is clear that the mobilization in the struggle for landownership has other origins besides CEBs. It has been suggested that CEBs give people a religious legitimation for preexistent motivations and aspirations for social changes and that the politicization of CEB members happens only when there are clear social conflicts (Novaes 1984). The mobilization does not emerge merely from religious work; other factors, parallel to CEB activities, are also responsible for political mobilization. In contrast to Pentecostalism, the CEBs have attracted people who had previous political and social concerns, as occurred with Margarida, Alice, and Aninha whose interviews were mentioned earlier.

Political actions do not bring immediate benefits to the poor (Lancaster 1987a, b); these benefits come only with time. In Alto do Carneiro and Alto José do Pinho, the organization of CEBs has brought some positive changes. Alice mentioned the struggle for electricity and water in Alto do Carneiro. She also referred to the partial victory this community won in obtaining landownership titles. Lúcio, Odete, and Ernestina described the public school as the most important victory of their CEB in Alto José do Pinho. The struggle for landownership was also cited, although it is not part of the CEB fight, as was the struggle for the school. Aninha also stressed the importance of CEBs in improvements for her area. She said that some people complained because their neighborhoods were not as urbanized as hers. She explained to them that every improvement in her area was obtained through people's struggles.

In summary, the progressive faction in the Catholic church tries to help poor people through political activities. It supports political movements in two ways: First, through the various specific *Pastorais*, it offers technical help; and second, through CEB religious reflection groups, it develops social and political awareness. The data show that political struggles supported by CEBs have been successful in the areas researched. The neighborhoods obtained some material improvements. CEBs used political tools for the material improvement of the poor community, and people from different religious groups benefited from these improvements. CEBs intend to eliminate clientele political behavior and individual abuse of power.

RELIGION AND POLITICS
AMONG THE POOR

Religious groups may be politically useful for survival, not only by acting as interest groups in the process of political patronage, but also by supporting social movements and motivating people to participate in them. The progressive Catholic church sees poverty as a political problem and attempts to help the poor by supporting political movements. It offers technical aid to these movements through the various *Pastorais* and attempts to develop social and political awareness in people through the CEBs.

In contrast, Pentecostalism and Afro-Brazilian religions do not want to change the clientele political pattern. Their political behavior is similar. Nevertheless, in my research, Pentecostals did not report personal experiences of patronage help. Unlike Pentecostals, some Afro-Brazilian people did have this experience or mentioned expectations of patronage support.

Pentecostals stress the apolitical aspect of their worldview and the importance of politically supporting a fellow believer; Afro-Brazilian Spiritists do not have a homogeneous opinion about politics. They seem not to have a political ideology that involves collective interests. Instead, they defend only their personal interests.

The fundamental element of political action by the three groups is economic survival. Each religious ideology supports a different view. Pentecostals stress the importance of choosing political candidates who share their religious identity (Protestant) because they will be honest and will defend the group's interests. Afro-Brazilian Spiritism are concerned with individual improvement and defending individual interests. CEBs stress the need for social transformation by trying to defend class interests and to create an identity for the poor.

CHAPTER VI

Cultural Strategies for Coping with Poverty

When Creuza, a Pentecostal woman from Rio de Janeiro, decided to start saving to buy a house, she barely earned enough money on which to survive. Her husband, had opposed her savings plan and told her that she could never save enough money to buy a house. She did not listen to him, however, because she believed God would help her. Creuza's faith in God's power enabled her to save the money. Her case illustrates how religious faith can help poor people survive or can motivate them to adopt functional behaviors and endure or overcome poverty. The creation of functional lifestyles can be useful as a cultural strategy in poor people's attempts to improve their lives.

To stress the role of religion as a catalyst for motivation does not imply that people's beliefs and behaviors are totally independent of their social positions. Nevertheless, it acknowledges a certain degree of autonomy of culture, religion, and values from the economic and social structure. This autonomy helps us to understand why people in similar economic and social positions adopt different behaviors.

For most people, religion tends to be more useful as a source of motivation than as a source of material income or power. In general, as we saw in earlier chapters, religious leaders are the only people who support themselves through the financial resources generated by religious groups. For most poor people, religion is a means of supporting politically and economically advantageous behavior or an aid in avoiding the psychological disintegration or apathy created by poverty.

Cultural strategies may motivate people to work and save, possibly stimulating individual and family upward mobility. They may also motivate people to participate politically and fight for community improvements. Various kinds of cultural strategies for coping with poverty are put forth through the different attitudes and behaviors encouraged by Pentecostalism, CEBs, and Brazilian folk religion. In this sense, the Protestant ethic, as described by Weber (1958), with its view of work as a religious calling and its emphasis on savings, can be considered a successful cultural strategy for upward mobility in early capitalism.

The question whether Latin American Pentecostalism creates a new Protestant ethic and transforms Latin Americans' attitudes toward working and saving has attracted the attention of many researchers.[1] Some studies have neglected the analysis of non-Pentecostal economic behaviors and attitudes. To address this question properly, it is necessary to discuss what is happening with non-Pentecostals. It is also important to focus on people's actual behavior rather than on their theological work, the ideas of their leaders, and their opinions and ideal values. In addition to the distance between the values of ordinary people and those of their leaders, there are differences in the way people actually behave and their explicit values. There are also differences between the intentions and the results of their actions. Individuals do not always behave as they think they should.

Therefore, although these strategies depend on worldviews and values, the mere analysis of these values cannot in itself account for the cultural strategies they support. As Weber remarked in relation to Calvinism, the ethic adopted by ordinary church members in their everyday lives is very different from the values defended by theologians.

ATTITUDES TOWARD WORK

As we observed earlier, people with different religious affiliations place an equally high value on work. For all of them, work is a way to obtain money, as well as a source of human dignity. To be called a "hard worker" is appreciated as a compliment from others and a form of self-definition. Spiritists (Graças, Maria, João, and José), traditional Catholics (Faustina and Clemente), CEB members (Maria Omar, Aninha, and Margarida), and Pentecostals (Creuza, Neusa, and Edson) all define themselves as people who like to work. All these people began their working lives very early, and they are proud of this fact.

Nevertheless, Pentecostalism differs from the other religions because it relates economic and work success to God's blessing. At the theoretical level, it presents a religious work ethic that is not found in other religions among the poor. This work ethic, however, is transformed at the practical level of everyday life. Pentecostalism simply provides its followers with a religious meaning to their search for jobs and security. They seem not to develop any special motivation toward work or entrepeneurship because of it. In general, Pentecostals' attitudes toward work and work behavior are similar to those of non-Pentecostals, and they do not change after conversion. Most Pentecostals I interviewed said their attitudes toward work and their desire for improvement did not change after they joined Pentecostalism.

People's attitudes in relation to work seem to depend less on their religious values and more on their experience in the job market, where everyone faces difficulties in finding employment. Almost all of the older interviewees, for example Lúcio (CEB), Sebastião (Assembly of God), and Luís (Spiritist), described a long period of unemployment in their lives, and the differences in their religious affiliation did not seem to decrease or increase the likelihood that they would experience years without regular employment and income. Many of their children were unemployed and looking for jobs. These are the children of Maria, Graças, and Luís, Afro-Brazilian Spiritists; Ilze, a traditional Catholic; Maria Omar, a CEB member; and Celeste, a Pentecostal from the Assembly of God in Recife. Others were working in jobs for which they are overqualified and are looking for new positions. These people have accepted low-paying or exploitative jobs for lack of anything better. Ilze, for example, would like to leave her job because her boss never pays her for the extra hours she works, but she cannot find another place to work. Despite her education, Socorrinho can find nothing better than a housekeeper's position. She can earn more as a housekeeper than at other employment only because she saves money on food and board. Edson, a Pentecostal, would like to have a job that does not require him to work on Sundays.

Most people, including Pentecostals, do not view work as their major religious calling, given the difficulty of finding any job and the even slighter chance of finding a good one. Although they value work morally and consider it important in their lives, some interviewees felt that work distracted people from God's service. This attitude is true not only for CEB members but for Pentecostals as well.

Some Pentecostals I interviewed had left their paying jobs in order to dedicate themselves to religious activities.[2] Although this behavior seems to be a sign of otherworldliness or a weak work ethic among Pentecostals, it is, in fact, an adaptation of their work ethic to the reality of their lives, an attitude that serves as a survival strategy. It allows people to avoid occupations that pay very little. Both Juca and Arnaldo left their jobs in order to dedicate themselves to the church. At the time they left work, they both also discovered they had heart problems. Juca's work had been physically very demanding, while Arnaldo's job had caused great emotional stress. In both cases, the jobs were not compatible with their health problems. If Juca and Arnaldo had not left their jobs, they might have become even more ill or even have died.

These reasons for leaving work cannot be considered to be signs of an otherworldly orientation. Passive behavior is not always an indication of social withdrawal or otherworldliness. It can be one means of struggling. In certain situations, passivity and submission can be efficient means of survival. Pentecostalism, in these cases, becomes a strategy of coping with poverty because it legitimates an option that seems economically irrational but that is functional for individual survival.[3] Passivity among Pentecostals is often a mere tactic; where the possibility of improving exists, there is no need for an escapist attitude. Although Edson, a twenty-year-old black Pentecostal, regrets his need to work on Sundays because it keeps him from Sunday services and Sunday school, he attends night services during the week instead of quitting his job. None of the interviewees left jobs that were not too stressful for them.

In summary, the shortage of jobs, coupled with the low-paying and exploitative situations of employment, prevent poor people of any religion from attributing a religious meaning to their work. Religion seems not to have much effect on the work ethic. Those who are most motivated to work do not share similar religious values or experiences. Nor is there any shared religious preference among those who place a lower value on work.

ATTITUDES TOWARD SAVING

Saving is equally valued by poor people regardless of their religious affiliation. Most poor people save or try to save, even if they sometimes must sacrifice such basic needs as housing, medicine, or food. Choosing less expensive food in order to save money is a strategy used by Creuza (a Pentecostal from Rio de Janeiro), and João (a Spiritist from Recife). João explains, "When bread is expensive, I just eat *macaxeira* [sweet cassava] instead."

Poor people create mechanisms to force themselves to save, such as the practice called *sorteio* (raffle), which is popular in Recife. A group of ten people, for instance, commits themselves to contributing a certain amount of money for ten months. Each month, there is a drawing of names, and the total amount is given to the person whose name is drawn. Ilze, a traditional Catholic, and Aniceto and Alice, CEB members, participate in *sorteios*. Ilze says this is the only way she can save money. Because of her commitment to the group, she makes any sacrifice that is necessary to pay into the *sorteio* each month. Aniceto likes the social aspect of the *sorteio*. He says, "It is also a meeting for friendship." Alice says her CEB organized *sorteios* when people needed money to install electricity. People are aware of the disadvantages of the system, given Brazil's high inflation. But they still prefer the *sorteio*, instead of saving money in a bank, because the minimum required to open a savings account is often beyond their means. Pentecostals do not mention the practice of *sorteio*. When asked directly, Eurídice, a Pentecostal from Recife, says she considers the *sorteio* to be a form of gambling, which is not acceptable in her religion. I found a similar strategy among the poor in Rio de Janeiro, but instead of drawing a name to receive the money each month, the group puts the money in a bank saving account or lends it at interest to one of the group in need. In some areas of Rio de Janeiro this method is called *caixinha* (small box). Pentecostals also participate in *caixinhas*.

Other people force themselves to save by asking someone else to keep their money for them. By doing so, people avoid spending the money on their everyday needs and force themselves to consume less. This is the practice of Socorro (a CEB member) and Maria (a Spiritist). Both ask friends who live in other neighborhoods to hold the money they want to save. Maria says this keeps her from buying items that are nonessential.

Women appear to save money more than men do. Severina and Creuza sometimes hide money from their husbands in order to save it. João also acknowledges this tendency to spend money and explains that in order to save money he gives almost all of his earnings to his wife. João notes that many of his male neighbors waste a lot of money in bars.

The most important goal of saving is to build or buy a house. Regardless of one's religious affiliation, to own a place to live is a definite aspiration of all. Interviewees saved even to obtain a shanty in a squatter settlement or an "invaded land."[4] Homeowners are very proud of themselves, and the acquisition of a house is very important in people's lives. Building a house is a lifelong project that frequently involves one's entire family, and is sometimes carried on by the children. The dream of Celeste's son is to obtain enough money to help his parents finish their house.

Building a house seems to take forever; Beto's house has been under construction for eight years. Generally, the houses are first made of wood or clay (*taipa*). Gradually, the owners substitute bricks and tiles. Construction materials are bought as soon as people have the money for them and are stocked in their home until they can afford to begin construction. People understand the problems of inflation and save money by investing in goods. The houses of Zefinha, Socorro, Beto, Conceição, and Neusa are visibly in the construction process. Many people, such as Neusa and Socorrinho, refer to future improvements they are planning for their houses.

CEBs try to expand the individual goal of owning a house into a collective project. Most of the slums and poor neighborhoods are squatter settlements where poor people do not own the land (Moura 1988). The Catholic church, through CEBs and other religious groups, such as the *Pastoral da favela*, perform an important role in helping poor people fight for land on which they can build houses or where they already have houses. Aniceto and Socorro obtained the titles for their plots through their local CEBs. Aniceto remembers that this religious group helped five or six people in the area to build their houses. And Rita once received money to help rebuild her house after it collapsed.

Despite having the same motivation to own a home, Pentecostals do not apply any religious meaning to this goal. Some Pentecostals benefit from victories in the struggle for land-ownership obtained through political movements supported by CEBs, but they do not emphasize this point in interviews or give religious meaning to this acquisition. Only Creuza provided a religious meaning to the project of building her house. She explained that God helped her to save money, to learn by herself how to build a house, and to pass on the knowledge of bricklaying and foundation laying to her neighbors. She also helped two fellow believers to construct their houses.

Many people have a religious goal in their saving, besides obtaining or improving their houses. For instance, Luís's wife, an Afro-Spiritist, has saved for ten years to "make her saint," a religious obligation in Afro-Brazilian Spiritism. Aniceto, who participates in a CEB, sometimes saves in order to travel to Juazeiro do Norte, a popular place for Catholic pilgrimages in the Northeast. Creuza is saving because she wants to travel in order to convert people to her Pentecostal church, as she did during her last visit to her parents' home in Paraíba, a state in northeastern Brazil. Pinça plans to use her savings to build a restroom for her Afro-Spiritist center.

My data do not show that Pentecostals save more or have more instrumental uses for their savings than people from other religions. But the Pentecostal ethic seems to be more supportive of savings than the ethic fostered by the other religious groups analyzed. In Brazilian society, where resources are scarce and the economy is unpredictable, it is almost impossible to find support for saving in a secular ethic. Pentecostalism may help the poor to save in three different ways. First, it explicitly values saving. An illustration of this fact is a quotation from Lesson 7 of the booklet *Lições Bíblicas* (Biblical Lessons), used in the Sunday school of the Assembly of God: "Saving is not synonymous with stinginess, as to waste money is not a sign of richness." In this lesson there is an interpretation of a part of the Gospel showing that Jesus also valued saving. In this respect, Pentecostalism differs from Catholicism (traditional or progressive) and from Afro-Spiritism, or any kind of Spiritism, because Pentecostalism gives religious meaning to saving and explicitly values it.

The second way Pentecostalism may encourage saving is through its emphasis on asceticism. Manoel, a Pentecostal of Alto José do Pinho in Recife, explains, "The leisure of the believer is to work." Pentecostals are not supposed to spend their money on "vanities." Creuza says her faith "curbed her vanity" as she learned to control her desire to buy clothing. Protestant groups in general also have an anticonsumption attitude. Lenice, who was raised as a Baptist, acknowledged this value in her former church. The third way in which Pentecostalism can reinforce saving is by offering hope and faith in the future. Saving supposes a belief in a predictable future. Pentecostalism may motivate people to save because it offers them confidence in the future through faith in God's plan. Crueza displays this attitude. Facing severe poverty, the nonreligious motivation to save is weak. For this reason, Pentecostals may save for a longer period of time than others.

Despite the fact that Pentecostalism does not change the motivation of its adherents in relation to production and work, it does seem to transform their attitudes about consumption. The Pentecostal ethic does not emphasize working more, but it stresses consuming less. This ethic is strategic for survival because it gives religious meaning to the survival strategy identified by Clark (1988) as "tightening one's belt," that is, reducing one's consumption to the bare minimum.

Most Pentecostals explain that they can meet their basic needs on their low incomes. The elimination of drinking alcohol, for instance, functions as a very important savings strategy. This confirms tendencies in which Pentecostals show different consumption patterns than people from other religious groups.[5] Pentecostal asceticism provides options to save through the reallocation of resources.

Poor people's life histories are mostly descriptions of searches for work and struggles to save and survive. Therefore, work and saving are important values for them. The Brazilian economy seems modern enough to require these values and behaviors from those who need to work to survive and who want to improve their lives. As in other modern societies, the Brazilian secular ethic shares aspects of the "spirit of capitalism."[6] Apparently, the alleged traditional hedonism of Brazilian culture has either been exaggerated in order to legitimate the exploitation of the poorest or is stronger in richer sectors of the society. Despite this fact, Pentecostalism seems to perform a role in motivating savings because when people face unemployment, health problems, and the impossibility of saving, the secular ethic loses its plausibility. Pentecostalism attempts to place this secular ethic in a religious context.

SUBJECTIVE EXPERIENCES

A person who wishes to adopt new cultural patterns of behavior needs not only an external structure of plausibility offered by the social support of other people who share the same values (Berger and Luckmann 1966) but also an internal plausibility structure bestowed by his or her own subjective experiences. Subjective experiences are not only the experiences resulting from the adoption of specific values. They are also the psychological consequences of people's actual interrelation and social practices in specific groups, organizations, and society. Accordingly, these experiences depend on the structure of religious movements as well as on people's values and ideologies.

Subjective experiences are the link between ideal intentions and values and actual practices. Depending on the social context and the organization of religious groups, the same religious views may generate different subjective experiences and consequently diverse behaviors. Different religions may also produce similar experiences. The analysis and comparison of the subjective experiences created by different religions are very important in understanding the role of these religions as cultural strategies to cope with poverty.

Two broad categories of subjective experiences are useful for coping with poverty: experiences that foster modernization or rationalization (in the Weberian sense) and experiences that strengthen solidarity among the poor. Experiences of renewal, of religious reflection, and of rejecting the dualism between private and public life that are shared by Pentecostals and CEB members, but not by the majority of Afro-Brazilian Spiritists and traditional Catholics, have this modernizing effect on people.

Experiences of Renewal

Pentecostalism and CEBs differ from folk religions with respect to the process of renewal that takes place in an individual's

life. This renewal means that a discontinuity occurs in the way
people view the world; that is, the individual experiences a conversion. This renewal experience is less common and evident
among CEB members and is more visible among Pentecostals.
Most CEB members do not seem to experience a conversion
because they have always been Catholic. But some say that their
experiences in CEBs has led them to change their previous conception of religion. Before becoming a CEB member, Odete,
a widow from Alto José do Pinho, was a participant of the
Catholic movement *Filhas de Maria* (Mary's Daughters). She
says that her participation in a CEB helped her see the importance of organizing people, which changed the way she viewed
religion and the community. Aurélio, who is sixty-eight, says
he viewed the Catholic church differently after participating in
the CEB of Alto José do Pinho, although he continued to organize pilgrimages to Juazeiro do Norte and was not considered
by the pastoral agents of his area to be an example of a conscien-
tious CEB member. Both Odete and Aniceto had experienced
a change, a discontinuity in their way of looking at religion
and at the world, which fostered a critical opinion of traditional
views.[7] This experience can be considered a form of conversion,
despite the fact that CEB members did not change churches or
dogmas as a result of participation in these groups.[8]

In contrast to the experiences of CEB members, the renewal
and conversion among Pentecostals is a far more dramatic experience. It is almost a rule for everyone, including some of
those raised in the faith. Interviews with Pentecostals produced
many descriptions of these experiences, most of them marked
by a miracle or a supernatural event, such as a cure.

The experience of conversion or alternation assumes a
questioning of the "world taken for granted" (Berger 1963).
Converts discover the limitations of the world based on the
common-sense view and thus become critical of it. Therefore,
Pentecostal's unequivocal respect for authority is often contra-
dicted by their real experience of criticizing tradition. Despite

their authoritarian values, some Pentecostals do not fear opposing authority if they perceive that authority as contradicting the Bible (Novaes 1985).

The convert goes through the experience of being able to choose his own religion, and traditionally the adoption of religion is not seen as a matter of choice. Afro-Brazilian Spiritists perceive their religious option as something innate to the individual, whereas Pentecostalism and CEBs require a conscious option from individuals. This requirement reveals a belief in the ability of the individual to change his or her life and therefore presupposes the ability to engage in nonfatalistic behavior.

The experience of renewal seems to support change and antitraditional values. Therefore, people who experience a renewal value personal changes as well as social change and political transformation. In both cases, valuing change is a useful means of coping with poverty.

Experiences of Religious Reflection

The experience of religious reflection is linked to the experience of renewal. Despite the presence of irrational factors in their conversion, Pentecostal and CEB members need a rational justification for the superiority of their faith, or of the new interpretation of their faith in the case of CEB members. The irrational elements only explain the initial attraction, whereas continuing participation requires arguments showing the universal truth of their religious beliefs and ethical requirements. Pentecostal and CEB members need to elaborate special justifications for their religious choices and lifestyles, since both fall outside the traditionally accepted one. Therefore they need religious reflection and knowledge. For example, although a miracle was decisive in Creuza's becoming a Pentecostal, she later studied the Bible in order to argue more convincingly that the Assembly of God was the true church. Helena experienced something similar. Although her conversion actually took place when her husband stopped drinking and she was healed, she frequently quoted the Bible during her interview to show the truth of her faith.

Among those interviewed, Pentecostals were admired for their religious knowledge. CEB members criticize traditional Catholics' ignorance of their faith. Odete, as a member of her CEB's baptism group, believes that people should study their religion in order to be baptized or to have their children baptized in the Catholic church. In her parish, if a person refuses to attend certain religious courses, he or she cannot be baptized, be a godparent, or have children baptized. Her priest explains that, as a result, there are only about fifty baptisms a year in his parish, whereas in areas where priests have a more traditional orientation, there are fifty baptisms a week.

Brazilian folk religious groups, the Afro-Brazilian Spiritists among others, emphasize specific behavior or ritual and place almost no emphasis on religious thought (Motta 1983). Afro-Brazilian Spiritists conceive an individual's religion as something innate, almost a natural predisposition. Maria, for instance, says she has had her religion from the time she was in her mother's womb. José's case is similar. He recalls that he had his religion as a child, even before he knew about the spirits. For Spiritists, some people are born with a certain spiritual power and are destined to become members or leaders of a Spiritist group. If they try to deny this fate, they may risk their lives. Conceição believes that her mother died because she became a Baptist Protestant, a *crente*, and no longer wanted to "work with the spirits" (*trabalhar com os espíritos*). For these people, religion is not a choice but a part of their personality and nature. Lula gives another illustration of this idea. Raised as a Protestant, Lula left his church as a teenager, but later in life, faced with serious problems, he asked for the help of an Afro-Brazilian Spiritist woman. This woman told Lula that he was a "man of the Bible" and that his life situation would improve only if he returned to a Protestant church.

In Afro-Brazilian religions, faith is legitimated by spiritual power. No intellectual reflection is needed to support the faith; experience with this power is enough. Therefore, people of these religions do not proselytize, but through their actions try to demonstrate the strength of their power. The same occurs in rural Catholicism (Mariz and De Theije 1991).

The Xangô (Pernambuco's name for an Afro-Brazilian religion) is a religion expressed through dancing, singing, and feeling, rather than through thinking (Motta 1983). This also seems to be the case with folk Catholicism. These religions do not emphasize reading or the use of words, whereas the reading of the Bible is fundamental in Pentecostal churches and CEBs, which are both verbal; words play an important role. In CEB meetings the use of written posters with slogans is common. There are also written phrases from the Bible on the front wall of almost all Pentecostal churches. Written words do not play an important role in traditional religions; there are no slogans in Afro-Brazilian Spiritist centers and traditional Catholic processions.

Pentecostals try to convert people by talking and reasoning with them. This attempt to convert by preaching assumes that people can choose their faith and lifestyle based on ideas. Therefore, despite their mystical or supernatural interpretation of reality, Pentecostals assume that religious affiliation is a matter of reason.

Because of the importance some religions place on the written word and a theoretical elaboration of faith, members are motivated to learn to read and to develop their speaking abilities. It is common to meet Pentecostals who affirm that they learned how to read as adults after their conversion to the Assembly of God. Although unsuccessful, Neusa, also from the Assembly of God, sought to become literate because she wanted to read the Bible. Motivated by her participation in a CEB, Benedita, a fifty-nine-year-old woman from Alto do Carneiro, still takes reading classes. Previous studies have shown that the CEB experience improves members' abilities to express themselves and formulate ideas and opinions (Duarte 1983; Petrini 1984). Pentecostals also develop public speaking skills through religious participation (Novaes 1985; Rolim 1985).

The stimulus for reading, speaking, and theoretical thinking can be useful not only in relation to an individual's social mobility but also for the organization of political movements. For this reason, despite their different values and ideologies, both Pentecostalism and CEB offer their members experiences that are advantageous in coping with poverty.

Experiences of Rejecting Dualism

Another rationalizing element that distinguishes CEBs and Pentecostalism from the traditional forms of religion in Brazil is their ethical emphasis. This emphasis, however, results only in different subjective experiences within the context of a kind of religious fundamentalism that rejects the dualism between private and public life. This dualism is "the heart of secularization and modernization" (Hunter 1989). In this sense, both CEBs and Pentecostal churches are bearers of fundamentalist religious experiences and critics of modern society. Paradoxically, although these groups reject secularization and modernization, both religions foster a rationalizing attitude toward life as a result of the ethic they adopt. The attempt to unite faith with life means that religion must change everyday life. Pentecostals perceive this change at the individual level; religious people must adopt a special lifestyle and morality. CEB members try to unite faith and life by using religious motivation and group action to solve day-to-day problems and engage in political participation.

Although they are religiously motivated, CEB participants do not embrace supernatural explanations for their everyday problems. These people explain and try to solve their problems without using sacred categories and means. Thus the CEB perspective, despite its rejection of the dualism of private and public life, is rational (in the Weberian sense) and is an aid to secularization. Despite their attempts to strengthen religion in society, CEBs are conducive to secularization because of their preference for the scientific and rational over the supernatural way of interpreting society and thinking in general.

Neither the emphasis on ethics nor the fundamentalist experience is present in the everyday expressions of Brazilian folk religions such as Candomblé or rural folk Catholicism. Yet some branches of these traditions may occasionally offer similar experiences. Umbanda, for instance, is ethical, and rural folk Catholicism has also created some ethical and fundamentalist religious movements.[9] The material and political consequences of these experiences depend, however, on the ethic stressed.

Within the second broad category of subjective experiences useful for dealing with poverty are those that strengthen solidarity and self-esteem among the poor and destroy the anomie and other negative psychological consequences of a situation of high deprivation. These experiences are shared, though not in exactly the same way, by Pentecostal churches, CEBs, and Afro-Brazilian Spiritists. They include community life, the possession of sacred knowledge, and the experience of power and dignity. Each experience has peculiarities that may lead to different consequences.

Experiences of the Supernatural

The possibility that ordinary people can be in touch with the supernatural world is a characteristic of almost all religions that are popular among the poor (Brandão 1980). The belief that any participant in a religious organization can deal directly with God fosters the development of a lay leadership and the development of small, autonomous groups. This belief also increases the self-esteem of the poor.

There is, however, a difference in the nature of the direct relationship to the supernatural among Afro-Brazilian Spiritists, Pentecostals, and CEB members. Afro-Spiritists and Pentecostals believe in the possibility of encountering the

supernatural through trances or trancelike states. In Pentecostalism, religious knowledge is accessible to anyone through
the study of the Bible, whereas sacred knowledge is a secret
available only to the leaders of Afro-Brazilian Spiritism (Prandi
1991).[10] Thus a direct relationship with the supernatural does
not necessarily lead to an equal access to revelation. This fact
was clearly expressed by Maria José when she explained her
preference for the Assembly of God. She is happier in this
church than she had been in the Afro-Brazilian Spiritist group
because she knows where to find religious truth. She can look
for it by herself in the Bible, whereas in Spiritism she had to
accept a religious leader's words.

The egalitarian possibility of revelation for all followers is,
therefore, another specific characteristic of CEB members and
Pentecostals, one that distinguishes them from members of traditional religions. The belief that followers of these religions are
directly inspired by God means that any participant of either
movement can feel competent to interpret the Bible, preach,
or become a leader. Both movements have a prophetic orientation, and members have access to revealed knowledge. Revealed
knowledge and the possibility of bypassing the mediation of
priests and saints in order to communicate with God are aspects
not only of the Pentecostal faith but of liberation theology as
well (Lancaster 1987a). Despite its rationalized discourse, the
basis of CEB knowledge is prophetic, revealed directly by God
(Macedo 1986).

Although CEB members share a prophetic orientation and
the possibility of direct revelation from God with Pentecostals,
the latter more often claim access to revealed knowledge. This
difference may be explained not only by Pentecostal experiences
with the Holy Ghost but also by the distinctive relationship
established between ordinary Pentecostal members and their
pastors and between CEB people and pastoral agents. Despite
holding democratic values and attitudes, some pastoral agents
may inhibit ordinary people's experience of religious revela-

tion and religious autonomy by their higher intellectual level and patronizing attitude. People who do not agree with their pastoral agents tend to leave their CEBs rather than organize themselves in opposition. Most behave as did a factory worker in Caxias Rio de Janeiro State; he disagreed with the ideas in his CEB and left the group without explaining his motives to anyone. Jorge, from another CEB of Caxias Rio de Janeiro, was an exception. He confronted the ideas of the priest and the other pastoral agents of his CEB. Jorge, however, was not from a poor class. He had a college degree and was the principal of a high school. According to one pastoral agent, Jorge's disagreements were related to his higher-class lifestyle and interests. I believe it was his higher educational level that allowed him to confront the priest. Lower-class people who disagree with a priest or pastoral agent may feel inhibited about confronting that person because they are less educated, are less familiar with the verbal debate that occurs in CEBs, and lack the intellectual resources necessary for this kind of confrontation. An example occurred during a debate on the voting procedures in decision making in a CEB in Rio de Janeiro. According to one pastoral agent, "the less politically conscious people" preferred a secret voting process, whereas "the conscious people" preferred a public vote. These preferences seem to be symptomatic of a hidden conflict. Could it not be that the "less politically conscious" people's preference for secret voting was a reflection of their need to feel less pressured to agree with the priests and pastoral agents? "Less politically conscious" is how pastoral agents describe poor people who do not agree with their views (Benedetti 1988).

Although Pentecostal churches also have internal conflicts and members who are unable to confront their pastors, the development of an opposition or the existence of a split seems common in these churches. These split-offs from the official church have often occurred within the Assembly of God in Brazil.

Experiences of Community Participation

Different religious groups foster diverse experiences of community life. CEB and Pentecostal church community experiences are similar because of the absence of marked social inequalities among the members of their community. By contrast, although their origins are among the poor, most Afro-Brazilian Spiritist centers include clients and members from higher economic strata of the society (Brown 1986).

When people from the same economic level participate together in small groups, they develop friendships as well as community consciousness and identity. As we have seen, they also form social support and self-help networks and develop group interests. In the case of CEBs, this consciousness reinforces the emphasis of the CEB view on collective work and the political conception of religion (Petrini 1984). Whereas Pentecostal churches do not share these values with CEBs, they do offer their own brand of community life and participation. Despite their emphasis on individualistic interpretations of society and religion, Pentecostals acknowledge that the maintenance of their faith and special lifestyle depends on community support and control. Therefore they strengthen their community activities and try to keep themselves relatively isolated from the rest of society.

The development of social networks of mutual support and the transformation of religious groups into political instruments are not phenomena limited to Pentecostal and CEB groups. They occur among Afro-Brazilian Spiritist groups as well. In the latter groups, however, people do not experience the same kind of CEB and Pentecostal community participation because the power of Afro-Brazilian Spiritist groups is concentrated in the hands of the leader. The community does not hold decision-making power; in addition, some of these groups are economically heterogeneous.

Experiences of Human Dignity

The strength of poor people's self-esteem is another strategic element for survival. Respect, among the people I researched, was an important value. These people normally address one another with respectful titles such as *dona, seu, senhor*, and *senhora*. This may be a way to cultivate the respectability and self-esteem threatened by their low socioeconomic status.[11]

Several authors have observed the feeling of dignity among Pentecostals.[12] There are different ways through which Pentecostalism helps the poor attain this feeling or strengthens their self-esteem. Strength may be gained by shifting emphasis from material richness to spiritual gifts, as Bobsin (1984) stresses, or by striving to construct the identity of a "decent person" (*gente de bem*).

Care taken over one's appearance is directly related to the construction of this identity. Zuleide decided to become a Pentecostal when she felt disrespected because of her indecent clothing. Pentecostal clothing also impressed and attracted Roxinha. In her first visit to the Assembly of God, Roxinha admired the women's modest dresses and long sleeves. In Pentecostalim one's appearance as a "good person" is closely related to actually being a "good person." The Pentecostals' attempts to differentiate themselves from the "world," or other poor people, seem to be a strategy for reinforcing self-esteem. Pentecostals perceive themselves as different and desire a feeling of distinctiveness and superiority. This attempt at differentiation is criticized by non-Pentecostals, who accuse Pentecostals of thinking of themselves as better than others. These were criticisms made by Afro-Brazilian Spiritists, such as João and Graças.

The appearance of decency and the conservative dress do in fact protect poor women from being treated like prostitutes and poor men from being considered thieves. As Gilkes (1985) shows, Pentecostal clothing also protects black women in the United States. Gilkes's opinion is shared by many Brazilian Pentecostals. Sebastião says the young Pentecostal woman's clothing serves as a form of protection. Neusa chose the word *armadura*, which means "armor," to refer to the sober clothing of a believer. Therefore, the very much criticized repressive aspects of Pentecostal morality [13] may play an instrumental role in supporting a respectful treatment of the poor and strengthening poor people's self-esteem.

CEBs help poor people learn not to be ashamed of their poverty (Macedo 1986; Petrini 1984). In CEBs the poor are God's chosen people. Pentecostals also believe they are chosen people, but they do not relate this fact to their poverty (Novaes 1985). In their view, chosen people are those who have accepted the Pentecostal doctrine. Both movements modify poor people's perception of themselves by instilling a sense of human dignity and self-esteem. This shift in self-perception is a necessary part of their search for improvement in life. It is important not only as a motivation for social mobility but for political participation as well.

Afro-Brazilian Spiritism also promotes human dignity and an increase in self-esteem; however, these attributes are more clearly perceived among the leaders and those who hold spiritual power than among ordinary members of the group. This high self-esteem is related very closely to experiences of supernatural power. Describing how often people from different social strata look for supernatural aid, Pinça and Graça, Afro-Spiritists from Recife, and José and Socorrinho, from Rio de Janeiro, are very confident of their importance. They know that rich people may need them because of their religious activities and power. The belief that they are "chosen" or specially gifted is clearly expressed, for instance, in Maria's, Pinça's, and José's accountings of their first supernatural experiences during their childhood.

Experiences with Power

Religion can be an important instrument in coping with poverty because it destroys poor people's experiences of being powerless. This sense of powerlessness is common among the very poor,[14] and most religions strive to overcome it with the belief in spiritual power and the possibility of performing miracles. Such is true of Pentecostalism and folk religion in Brazil.

CEBs have other ways of fighting against powerlessness. Rather than emphasize the power of miracles, CEBs stress the power of the unity of the poor. In contrast to Pentecostals and Afro-Brazilian Spiritists, whose life histories are full of miraculous healings or supernatural experiences and happenings, most CEB members do not mention supernatural experiences. CEBs do not offer solutions to individual health problems. CEB members mentioned health problems only as a factor that might prevent them from participating in religious activities.

Supernatural cures and miracles are very important for Afro-Brazilian Spiritists. They are the basis for the veracity of their religion. In addition, experiences with supernatural powers are more common among those who have no material power (Brown 1986). Therefore, through their spiritual power, the poor, blacks, and women not only strengthen their self-esteem but also obtain material benefits for their supernatural services.

For a Pentecostal, the cures for body and soul are the same (Kessel and Guerrero 1987). Faith is the key that heals everything. In this respect, Pentecostals hold a unified perception of the physical with the spiritual and take a psychosomatic approach to health problems. This approach acknowledges that psychological stress, family conflicts, and the frustrations created by poverty affect one's health. It also recognizes that these factors may be as unhealthy as the actual absence of food and hygiene.

Pentecostalism is a way of dealing with health problems and illnesses, which are the most personal and frequent expressions of misery (Fry and Howe 1975). The Brazilian poor need an efficient means to become healthy or, at least, to explain disease. Pentecostalism, like Afro-Brazilian religions, has been this means for many people. Both religions not only offer healing but also give meaning to illness and teach people how to live with it. Most religions do this. Nevertheless, Pentecostalism's emphasis on healing seems to be stronger because of its view that to convert is to heal. Neusa's story demonstrates the Pentecostal belief that illness may be a sign of the presence of evil. She had a fever on the day of her baptism, but the fever left her as soon as she was submerged under the baptismal water. The sacred water expelled the evil that had attacked her.

In addition, Pentecostalism emphasizes miracles and miraculous healing as missionary instruments. Healing attempts to show the truth of the Pentecostal faith. New members are converted through healing.[15] One of the missionary's jobs is to visit hospitals and pray for the sick, as Anésio and Roxinha, Pentecostals from Recife, did on a weekly basis. The healing power of Pentecostals is widely acknowledged, even by Graças, an *Umbandista* leader from Recife, who said that "*os crentes curam e como curam!*" ("Believers heal, and do they ever!").

Nowadays, the more traditional Pentecostal churches, such as the Assembly of God, face competition from new Pentecostal churches, such as *Casa da Benção*, (Blessing House) and *Igreja Universal do Reino de Deus*, (the Universal Church from God's Kingdom), which are very concerned with healing and exorcism and less concerned with fostering a new lifestyle (Rubim 1991). One Assembly of God pastor stressed that his church's perspective is different from that of churches that wanted to attract people simply to heal them and to earn money. Pastors from traditional Pentecostal churches warn their followers against the more recent churches that have no "doctrine," insinuating that the "miracles" they perform are not the work of the Holy Ghost. The growth of the new Pentecostal churches worries traditional Pentecostal churches, historical Protestants, and the Catholic church.

Miraculous healings are part of Pentecostals' everyday lives. Even those not attracted to this religion for health benefits report experiences of supernatural healing. Many of the healings were only partial healings, such as was true of the husbands of Creuza and Roxinha. Both men had survived heart attacks but still suffer from heart problems. Anésio is a similar case. He lists all the medicines he still must take, but he says he is cured by God because he can lead a normal life. Religion helps these people reorganize their lives in order to live with their diseases. Their belief that they received a special blessing, and that God's power is stronger than their illnesses, has an important role to play as a strategy for enduring hardship. The experience of being able to heal themselves with what they perceive to be the power of God destroys the feeling of powerlessness that is characteristic of the very poor.

A Pentecostal pastor acknowledged the power of faith as an explanation for the success of his religion among poor people, stating that his religion empowered them. This idea was echoed by Creuza, a Pentecostal, who felt that she could do everything with God's help and that nothing was really impossible for her.

A Sense of Coherence

In general, religion offers an experience of spiritual power to those who have no material power. Every day, miracles occur among Spiritists and Afro-Brazilian Spiritists. Some traditional Catholics also believe that people can attain seemingly impossible goals through prayer and *promessas* to the saints. They describe "miracles" they have experienced as well. Pentecostalism is not the only religion to help its followers overcome feeling of powerlessness. Pentecostalism is unique in that it interprets the miracles as part of God's plan. Pentecostals believe that only God can perform miracles. In this respect Pentecostalism is different from Afro-Brazilian Spiritism. Afro-Spiritists accept the existence of supernatural forces other than God that can also perform miracles. They do not believe there is a divine plan that rewards good people. For instance, Luís, an *Umbandista*, recounted that his first wife had died because she had disobeyed her saint. Conceição also believed her mother had died because she no longer wanted to work with the spirits. João referred to a man who died when he incorporated a spirit, and another who became ill due to spiritual encounters carried out by his enemies. Graças worried about one of her daughters, who liked to "work" with low spirits. The fear of the Afro-Brazilian Spirits' supernatural power is widely spread in Brazil and shared by people from different religious groups.

Because Pentecostals believe in God's Providence they feel protected from these forms of supernatural power. The important role this protection plays in attracting converts to Pentecostalism in Brazil has perhaps been underestimated.[16] The adoption of Christianity as a means of protection against magic was also observed by Weber (1972).[17] The protection against magic is related to the idea of Providence and the idea of a powerful God who has a plan for humanity (Thomas 1991; Weber 1972).[18] God is stronger than any magic, which loses its power because it exists outside God's plan and does not follow her rules. Therefore, the idea of God's plan weakens the power of magic. In this sense, God's plan performs a role in religion that is similar to the role that reason plays in science. In the scientific view, magic does not have power because it does not follow any logical rule.

CEB members do not appear concerned with the problem of African magic, or spells (*trabalhos feitos*, as it is called in Brazil). Though they may believe in the power of the Spiritists and spirits, they do not talk about them as do Pentecostals and others. In general, the CEB view and that of the pastoral agents avoid dealing with these questions.

In contrast with Afro-Brazilian Spiritism, Pentecostalism emphasizes the meaning of miracles and their relationship to God's will. Therefore, if a healing fails to occur, there must be some reason, a meaning to be ascribed. In Arnaldo's interpretation, the disease he suffered from was God's way of appealing to him to dedicate himself to religious work. Creuza interpreted her broken leg as an opportunity to witness God's power. Faith in a divine logic that guides and determines life offers a psychological advantage in the struggle for survival. An Israeli sociologist, Aaron Antonovsky (1979), identified what he called lawfulness, or a "sense of coherence," as the principal psychological element that differentiated people who were able to survive concentration camps and establish a relatively healthy life from those who never could make this adjustment.[19] Neusa's life illustrates how faith can give meaning to suffering and how religion can offer a "sense of coherence," helping one to endure a life of poverty and hardship. The faith in a divine Providence and its accompanying sense of lawfulness seem to be more useful as strategies for enduring poverty than is the feeling of power experienced with miracles. This argument can be illustrated by comparing two similar supernatural healings experienced by Creuza, a Pentecostal, and Clemente, a traditional Catholic. Clemente is convinced that because of his *promessa* to São Francisco de Canindé, his oldest son was cured of a fatal disease and did not die as a child. For her part, Creuza believes that her son died during a childhood illness but was brought back to life as a result of her prayers and faith in God. Both children had survived as a result of their parents' faith, but they were now alcoholic adults. Clemente regrets his *promessa* and feels responsible and guilty for his son's problems as an adult. He says his son would have suffered less if he had died as a child. Unlike Clemente, Creuza expects another miracle. She believes that God must want something from her son, since he restored him to life. These examples show how the attribution of meaning to suffering is more important as a coping strategy than the miraculous solution of an immediate problem. Lawfulness cannot be identified as fatalism. Compared to Creuza, Clemente could be considered a fatalist. He assumed that his son's fate was to be an alcoholic. But he lacked the sense of coherence that Creuza had.

Experience with the sense of coherence, in theory, is offered by any religious system. Although somehow implicit in all religious people's life histories, it is more evident in the life histories of Pentecostals and of the more sophisticated Afro-Brazilian Spiritists (those who hold a more systematic Kardecist view). It is also related to the process of religious rationalization.

Analysis of the potentialities of these experiences as tools to overcome poverty suggests that religion can be useful for the poor. Not only does it help them rationalize their behavior, but it also overcomes the anomie caused by misery.[20]

PENTECOSTALISM AND MOTIVATION
TO ENDURE POVERTY

In addition to the experiences already described, Pentecostalism motivates its adherents to especially useful behaviors in the process of coping with poverty, behaviors not encouraged by other religious groups. Specifically, converts to Pentecostalism become motivated to stop drinking alcohol and to take care of their families. Because of the situation of deprivation and the gender role in Brazilian society, these motivations are more frequently lacking among poor men than among poor women.

Alcoholism is one of the most serious problems among low-income Brazilians, and households headed by alcoholics seem to fall into the worst poverty level. Many of my interviewees had alcoholic relatives: Socorro's husband, Aniceto's son-in-law, and the sons of Clemente, Creuza, Roxinha, and Pinça, spent almost all their resources in drinking. Others, such as João's stepson, may or may not be considered an alcoholic, but drinking accounts for a great deal of his time and money.

For the most part, this behavior can be attributed to the difficulties of earning enough to make ends meet and the daily pressures this economic battle entails. Creuza's husband, for instance, began drinking after a long period of unemployment. Alcoholism further deteriorates an already precarious standard of living among the poor.

Pentecostal churches, as well as other Protestant churches—Baptist being the most frequently mentioned—motivate people to give up drinking alcohol. Although other strategies may be adopted (in Alto José do Pinho, Recife, for example, there was a successful Alcoholics Anonymous group), conversion to a Protestant church, or *Igreja de Crente* (Believer Church), seems to be perceived even by non-Pentecostals as an efficient, popular, and powerful antidrinking strategy among the poor.

Many male conversions are alcohol related. Sometimes the woman converts first and then tries to convert her alcoholic husband. As observed earlier, many Pentecostals tend to have very unstable economic situations before their conversions. Pentecostalism offers immediate solutions for these people. When people stop drinking, they can feel an economic improvement immediately. Accordingly, Edson, as well as Neusa's and Creuza's husbands, continue to be poor, but by not drinking, they alleviate some of their hardship.

Many non-Pentecostals admire believers because of this transformed behavior. Odete, a CEB leader, refers to a neighbor who used to drink and whose children always asked for food at Odete's house. After his conversion, this neighbor stopped drinking and found a job, thereby changing his life and those of his relatives.

EMPHASIS ON THE FAMILY

The number of single mothers is high among the poor population in Brazil. In Recife 32.6 percent of all families living in a particular poor neighborhood were headed by single females

(Scott 1988). Interviewees from the different religious groups had daughters or sisters who were single mothers. Although many of the women were widows, none was currently a single mother. Most of them, however, help a daughter or a sister. A typical case is Roxinha, now a married Pentecostal in her sixties, who was during her youth the single mother of six. Now she supports her youngest daughter, who is single and has a baby. The main support of a single mother is her own mother or her sisters.

In general, when a Pentecostal single woman becomes pregnant, she is expelled from her church, as happened with Socorro's sister. But she can convert to another Pentecostal denomination if she decides to restrict her sexual life. The Pentecostal emphasis on family life and strict sexual morality can be considered another motivational strategy for coping with poverty. A household where a couple is present means fewer economic problems and less instability than a single-parent family. By motivating paternal responsibility and trying to change male sexual attitudes (Santiago 1988), the moral doctrine of Pentecostalism has the potential effect of decreasing the rate of single motherhood and broken marriages, thus indirectly reducing further deterioration in the standard of living among poor families. Despite their opposition to scientific birth control methods, Pentecostalism's strict sexual morality forms a natural birth control. Pentecostal families are not necessarily larger than families of non-Pentecostals. Late marriages, such as Zezé's, also serve as a natural mechanism of birth control.

In contrast to Pentecostalism, CEBs do not emphasize the family problem (Burdick 1989), nor is sexual morality an important question at CEB meetings. Pastoral agents, in fact, tend to avoid these questions. Most of them criticize the religious emphasis on sexual morality as being a private, individual approach to religion. Moreover, they believe these questions are "middle-class preoccupations" and hesitate to impose middle-class values and sexual morality on the poor, preferring to let the poor define their own sexual morality. CEB members, however, hold a strong ethic in these matters. One interviewee told of a man and a woman from her CEB who each had been previously married to someone else in the Catholic church but both wanted to separate from their spouses and live together in a house built by the community. This union did not please the community. As a result, the community did not allow them to move in, and the couple lost their leadership position at their CEB. Another example was of a woman from a CEB who avoided taking Communion because she had not been married in the church, despite the fact that a pastoral agent from her area thought this was unnecessary.

All religions practiced by poor people offer subjective experiences that overcome the anomie created by misery and, as a result, serve to support the poor in enduring material deprivation. In analyzing the subjective experiences shared by Pentecostals and CEB members, however, it appears that religious experiences in these two groups may also foster a modern consciousness that is advantageous in the struggle for material survival and improvement in present-day Brazilian society. Therefore, of all the religions analyzed, Pentecostalism seems to offer more motivations that help the poor Brazilian individual to survive. In addition to the subjective experiences mentioned, it helps the poor endure poverty through its emphasis on the family and its fight against alcoholism.

Pentecostalism seems to be more instrumental than other religions as a tool for enduring poverty, rather than an instrument of upward mobility. Of all the religions analyzed here, it was the one that most encouraged people to face up to the frustrations created by the absence of material resources and the impossibility of increasing these resources.

CONCLUSION

The Brazilian religious arena has undergone important transformations in the past few decades. The hegemony of the Catholic church and traditional folk Catholicism has been shaken. Pentecostal churches have spread rapidly, while Afro-Spiritism and new religious movements have flourished. Religious diversity is a relatively recent historical phenomenon among Brazil's lower classes and is clearly represented by the presence of churches from various Protestant denominations and different Afro-Brazilian Spiritist centers.

Changes in Brazilian society and changes abroad are responsible for this new religious environment. The growth of CEBs and Pentecostalism in Brazil is related to changes in the international Catholic church. The innovations brought by Vatican II have had a direct impact on Brazilian religion. The *aggiornamento* of the Catholic church proposed by the Vatican II, as a process of rationalization and modernization of the Catholic church, included a lessening of emphasis on rituals, saints, and magic practices. These changes intensified the marginalization of the Brazilian poor in the Brazilian Catholic church, and Afro-Brazilian Spiritism and Pentecostalism became attractive alternatives for Catholics who missed the enchantment and magic in their religion. On the other hand, the CEBs emerged as an attempt to reach the poor, whom the Brazilian Catholic church was never able to integrate.

Another international factor that affected religion in Brazilian religious field was the missionary drive of Protestant denominations from the United States.

In addition to external factors, several internal elements of

Brazilian society have fostered the growth of new religions. The processes of industrialization and modernization have fostered a rationalization of life in its different aspects, as well as a change in the Brazilian religious arena. The growth of Afro-Brazilian Spiritism and Pentecostalism does not represent a negation of Weber's hypothesis of a process of religious rationalization in industrializing societies, but reflects a rationalization in the Brazilian religious field as a whole. Despite their enchanted worldview and emotionalism, Pentecostalism and the new forms of Afro-Brazilian Spiritism, such as Umbanda, are relatively more rationalized religions than traditional Afro-Brazilian Spiritism and folk Catholicism. They embrace a moral ethic and adopt an intellectual systematization of their faith and bureaucratization of their institutions.

Although a structural analysis helps us understand the transformations of Brazilian religions, it is insufficient to convey the diversity of people's practices in their everyday lives. People in the same structural position may opt for different religions, and individuals may develop specific practices that are not structurally predictable. In order to understand what causes religious transformations in Brazil it is also necessary to understand the role of each religious group in people's everyday lives.

Most of the Brazilian population are poor. As poor people, their main concern is their fight against poverty and for survival. This concern pervades all aspects of their lives. The economic needs of poor people strongly affect their lifestyles and the organization of their groups. The analysis of how a poor family copes with economic hardships shows that religions popular among the poor tend to perform an important role in their struggle to overcome poverty and survive. An analysis from the standpoint of poor individuals and families is useful for understanding not only religious change but also cultural changes and changes in values that occur during the fight against poverty at the level of small groups. Human beings are symbolical beings, so survival and fighting against poverty are not merely eco-

nomic or physical problems but also a cultural one. It requires
not only artifacts, or the material culture, but also motivations
and meanings. As a source of meaning, religion is fundamental in an individual's daily struggle to survive and improve his
or her life. But religious influences on coping with poverty include other dimensions besides the symbolical, motivational,
cognitive, and normative ones. Religious groups and institutions may be transformed into alternative means of obtaining
material goods and power. All religions of the Brazilian poor
seem to be, at both the subjective and objective levels, related
to the poor's struggle for survival. Despite holding distinctive organizations and worldviews, all religious groups that are
popular among the poor are materially useful. Therefore, religion does not always prevent people from fighting for their
interests, as Marxist theory argues. On the contrary, the religions of the Brazilian poor tend to support the poor's struggle
for a better life and for survival.

Despite the material functionality of religion, people's religions are not economically determined. No one chooses a religion because of its material advantages. Instead, religion is basically a source of meaning (Berger 1969). Thus a functionalist
model does not offer an appropriate explanation for religious
phenomena.

The Brazilian poor lack institutional supports. The welfare
state, political parties, and unions are weak institutions among
Brazil's low-income population. At the objective level, religions
in Brazil have helped the poor by offering them some alternative support groups and by fostering their demands for modern
welfare state protections. At the subjective level, religions create special motivations to endure poverty that secular society
has not offered.

Strategies offered by each religious group differ from one
another according to their means of action. Cultural or motivational strategies help people solve their problems only by changing their values and motivations, or their subjective reality.

Religious groups also use material and political strategies and resources to support people in their struggle for survival. In these strategies, the objective or institutional dimension of religion performs an important role. But the type and efficacy of the material support offered to the poor by each religious groups vary. CEBs offer strategies for coping with poverty that are more useful to the poor community as a whole, rather than to individuals. By contrast, Pentecostalism fosters strategies that better support individuals, especially those who face personal crises. CEB and Pentecostal strategies for coping with poverty tend to be more adjusted to the situation of the poor in modern and industrial society than are strategies used by traditional folk religions or nonromanized Catholicism.

Despite their use of institutional and material means, these strategies are rooted in values and religious views. The objective and subjective aspects of religion are interconnected in all strategies. The analysis of the religious views and each religious group's strategies helps us understand the different appeals of each group and the distinctions between the people each group attracts. Brazilians attracted to CEBs tend to be people who were able to overcome survival crises, and, although poor, they are better off economically than others in their community. In contrast, people convert to Pentecostalism when they are experiencing a life crisis. Pentecostalism has proved to be an efficient strategy for overcoming these crises, and therefore for supporting the poorest people.

CEBs have a weaker appeal among the population than Afro-Brazilian religions and Pentecostalism. The data suggest different explanations for this fact. The first explanation is that the CEB perspective is difficult for the Brazilian poor to understand fully and accept because it implies a redefinition of some basic cognitive assumptions of these populations. The second reason is economic; that is, CEBs do not offer immediate solutions to problems of poverty. The poorest of the poor have a greater need for the immediate support offered by Pentecostalism and Afro-Brazilian Spiritism and therefore engage less often in CEBs.

The comparison between Pentecostal and CEB worldviews suggested that they represent different expressions of religious rationalization. Both views thus constitute ruptures with the traditional folk Catholic tradition and Afro-Brazilian Spiritism; however, the Pentecostal rationalization is more limited than that of the CEBs. Moreover, Pentecostal rationalization affects only the life of the individual. According to Pentecostalism, individuals can choose their destiny by accepting God or not. Individuals are responsible for their personal problems, but not for those of society. By contrast, CEBs view social life as dependent on people's organizations, attitudes, and decisions. Therefore, the CEB rationalization supports collective activities.

CEBs break the basic cognitive assumptions of Brazilian folk religions, and because of their different definition of reality, they propose a rupture with some values of the traditional religions as well. Cognitive assumptions and values are responsible for the CEB preference for strategies that contradict the logic of the traditional system. Although Pentecostalism also breaks with folk religions, its main rupture is normative. Pentecostalism proposes a universal and restrictive ethical code. Because of the individualistic character of this ethic, the introduction of the universalistic principle by Pentecostalism does not affect Pentecostal political practices and attitudes, but only members' individual behaviors. As a result, Pentecostal people will innovate only at the subjective level, or on a level that uses motivational or cultural strategies to cope with poverty. Pentecostal institutional and group strategies to cope with poverty tend to be similar to those of traditional religious groups.

Pentecostalism and Afro-Brazilian Spiritism become sources of income for their leaders. Although Pentecostal churches are composed primarily of poor people, they tend to be enriched as institutions. Pentecostalism values religious spending, and

Pentecostal people regularly give money to their church. Afro-Brazilian Spiritist leaders also may earn higher incomes in relation to their neighbors or people from the lower sectors in general. CEBs do not offer any paying positions to their local leaders. In fact, the leaders' positions may result in material disadvantages. Local CEB leaders who are devoted full-time to community and religious works tend to be housewives or retired or unemployed people—people without jobs. Pentecostalism and Afro-Spiritism generate resources for their leaders, whereas CEBs search for the material improvement of the community as a whole. The material strategies offered by CEBs are more collectively oriented.

As religions composed almost exclusively of the poor, Pentecostal churches and CEBs do not ascribe a strong spiritual meaning to charity; instead, they attempt to change the traditional religious meaning of charity. These religious groups do not view the poor, or themselves, as objects of charity. In this respect they differ from Kardecist Spiritism, Umbanda, and traditional Catholicism, which are religions that embrace people from different social classes.

Another material strategy that occurs in all religious groups is the creation, in most cases unintentional, of networks of mutual material support. These networks are alternatives to the traditional kin and neighborhood networks—they do not attempt to replace them. Religious networks have a broader dimension than those composed of kin and neighbors and are therefore more advantageous. Through their religions, the poor are able to contact people from different areas of the city, different regions of the country, and even people from abroad. In addition, they may establish contact with people from other social classes.

None of the religions analyzed ascribed a redemptive meaning to poverty. None of my interviewees considered their deprived economic situation a spiritual advantage, nor did they ascribe any other religious meaning to being poor. Indeed, Brazilian poor people reject poverty and want to improve, seeing poverty in every aspect as a negative and something to be overcome and differing only in the way they struggle for improvement. Despite considering the poor as chosen people, CEBs view poverty as an injustice or sin that must be fought. Because they are the victims of this injustice, the poor are chosen by God to head this fight.

Despite being similar in theory to the Protestant ethic described by Weber, the new individual moral ethic proposed by Pentecostalism in everyday practice differs from Weber's ideal type in some ways. The current Brazilian job market seems to hinder the development of the perception of work as a calling among Pentecostals. Nevertheless, most people, irrespective of their religious affiliation, value work and saving. These findings contradict the stereotype that poor people in general and the poor Brazilian in particular do not value work and saving. Brazilian poor people seem to be very motivated to work and save, and although they do not relate work with economic success, these people do see work and saving as a moral value. Pentecostal economic values do not differ from those of most of the poor population in Brazil. As Weber (1958, 72) remarks, a social economic organization imposes its own values by punishing with economic failure those who do not adopt them and rewarding with material success those who do adopt them. An economic rational lifestyle and holding work and saving in high esteem are important values in Brazilian society. Brazilian society has not materially rewarded all those who have embraced these values. The life experience of the poorest Brazilians, even during the golden years of "the Brazilian miracle," never offered plausibility to such values. In the past few years economic depression and high inflation have shaken these values for the society as a whole even more. While the Brazilian Pentecostal ethic attempts to reinforce dominant modern capitalist values, ascribing religious meaning to them, no strong influence of religion on people's economic practices was observed.

The analysis of motivational strategies shows that Pentecostalism offers motivations for cultural transformations in individuals' private lives or family lives, while CEB proposes a transformation in the public sphere or political attitudes. Nevertheless, all religious groups composed of the poor are engaged in politics. This is understandable because poverty in Brazil is also a political problem. Therefore, what is new in CEBs is not their mixture of religion with politics. The novelty of CEBs is the type of politics that they engage in, and the religious meaning they ascribe to political actions. Despite being active in politics, Pentecostals tend to devalue political activities. They do not ascribe any religious meaning to these activities. The Afro-Brazilian Spiritist groups have similar attitudes and behaviors.

CEB innovations represent the adoption of more universalist values in politics. CEBs do not aim to exchange votes for benefits for individual people or the community but to request improvement as a universal right for all the poor. They also try to defend the ideological vote and change the political patronage attitude.

Despite the differences in the motivations intentionally fostered by CEBs and Pentecostal churches, the comparative analysis of the subjective experiences these religions offer to their members has led me to advance the hypothesis that the long-term political consequences of Pentecostalism and CEBs will not be very different. The consequences and intentions of people's behaviors are not always consistent. Weber's analysis of the Protestant ethic calls attention to the unintended consequences of religious attitudes. A pastoral agent interviewed was aware of the gap between the church's intentions and the results of its actions and said, "Probably the CEBs will not in the future be what we predicted in the past." The comparison of the subjective experiences offered by the participation in Pentecostal churches and CEBs has suggested that despite the different intentions and worldviews of each group, there is a high probability that the Brazilian CEBs and Pentecostal churches will have similar unintended consequences. In different ways, both help the poor to cope with poverty and adjust to the new class relationship and the modern state in Brazil.

The Brazilian progressive Catholic church's use of religion as a tool to deal with the problems of poverty is not original. Folk Catholicism, Afro-Brazilian religions, and Pentecostalism also offer the poor support for their economic survival. CEBs and Pentecostalism, however, offer innovative strategies that are similar. These similarities heretofore, however, have been underestimated in most comparisons between CEBs and Pentecostalism; among such studies are those of Francisco Rolim (1980) and Jether Ramalho (1977). Despite opposing political views, CEBs and Pentecostal religious proposals share important characteristics and may in the long term lead to similar changes of attitude and behavior among the poor.

Most earlier literature, in fact, has failed to perceive the rationalizing role of the Pentecostal view. Many authors believe that Pentecostalism merely imitates a traditional relationship to authority and the supernatural and does not represent Pentecostalism, among other things, as a process of rationalization. This literature makes the assumption that the ideal values expressed by a people's speeches are the determinants of behavior. It also makes the false assumption that the Pentecostal emphasis on individual improvement prevents an engagement in the struggle for social and political transformations, as advocated, say, by CEBs. This premise of an opposition between individual economic improvement and motivation to engage in social transformation is doubtful. Pentecostal and CEB processes are similar insofar as they express a kind of religious rationalization, and insofar as that process engenders a cultural and political autonomy among the disenfranchized. The difference between the CEBs and Pentecostalism is the degree to which they offer rationalization and autonomy of organization, and that, notwithstanding their basic political views and values, the degree of rationalization and the degree of autonomy of their organizations are the most important determinants of the attitudes and behaviors of their followers.

These processes of rationalization, cultural change, and organization of the poor are not irreversible or revolutionary in practice; rather, they are part of a complex process of the political and economic transformation of Brazilian society. The cultural transformation and organization of the poor, as part of this broad process, can nevertheless affect the destiny of Brazilian society, while still being dependent on the larger trends of the society as a whole.

NOTES

Introduction

1. Life expectancy in Brazil is sixty-five years, and the mortality rate among children less than one year old is 6.7 percent (Valle Silva 1991).
2. Vilmar Faria (1991, 34) notes that he is also aware that other factors, such as the traditional way to change votes by benefits, may have affected the expansion of social benefits.
3. Hélio Jaguaribe et al. (1986) observe that the enactment of reformist political measures requires social and political support, which depends on the values and ideological positions of the different groups in Brazilian society.
4. I adopt Clifford Geertz's (1975) concept of and approach to culture, which emphasizes its symbolic role of ascribing meaning.
5. I am not arguing again Oscar Lewis's theory of the culture of poverty, which has already been criticized (Leacock 1971; Leeds 1971; Valentine 1968).

Chapter I

1. According to the data collected by the Fundação Instituto Brasileiro de Geografia e Estatística, or IBGE (1990), this rate would be 26 percent.
2. Madeleine Adriance (1986) shows that in the last three decades the absolute number of nuns, brothers, and lay brothers has decreased in Brazil. In 1965 there were 40,141 sisters, 1,932 brothers, and 1,811 lay brothers; in 1981 there were 37,691 sisters, 1,395 brothers, and 1,082 lay brothers.
3. Riolando Azzi (1991), Heraldo Maués (1987), and Marjo De Theije (1990) describe the difficulties and conflicts the "romanization" created.

163

4. People from rural areas hardly accept the romanization that attempts to rationalize Catholicism. In this respect, Brazilian peasants can be considered less religious than people from the cities. The exceptions are peasants who immigrated from Europe in the nineteenth and twentieth centuries. Weber's (1972, 80–84) analysis of the religiosity of peasants is helpful toward understanding the difficulties of the Roman Catholic church in being accepted in the Brazilian countryside. Weber (1972, 83) remarks that only in modern times, when the process of rationalization became a threat to religion, did peasants become "a distinctive prototype of the pious man." This observation explains the distinction between Catholicism among rural people from southern Brazil (immigrants from Germany, Italy, and Poland) and those of the rest of the country, especially in the North and Northeast.

5. Antoniazzi (1989) writes that some authors estimated that 15 percent of Catholics are romanized and suggests this proportion might be higher (20 percent) if one identifies romanization with attendance at Sunday Mass. I think 20 percent is an overestimation of this group because some people do, indeed, go to Mass and do not internalize the ideas and attitudes of official Catholicism.

6. Daudelin (1991) believes that José Comblin's (1987) estimate of 4 percent of the Catholic population and Alberto Antoniazzi's (1989) estimate of 5 percent are still high. Daudelin estimates CEB membership at most at only 250,000 people, which is less than .5 percent of the total Catholic population.

7. Studies by Laura Duarte (1983), Gustavo Castro (1987), and Luíza Fernandes (1985) are examples of research concerned with the educational role of CEBs.

8. A special number of the journal *Comunicações do ISER* 9, no. 39, was dedicated to discuss this crisis.

9. For instance, the successor to the progressive D. Hélder Câmara at the Archdiocesis of Olinda and Recife is now the conservative archbishop D. José Cardoso Sobrinho.

10. Although the Fundação Instituto Brasileiro Geogragia e Estatística (1990) data indicate that 5.9 percent of the total religious population, 5.85 percent of Catholics and 21 percent of Afro-Brazilian Spiritists participate in more than one religion, I found in a poor neighborhood in Recife that about 11

percent of Catholics also attended Afro-Brazilian cults (Mariz 1992). This religious *bricolage* is observed when a large proportion of Catholics believe in reincarnation (Carneiro and Soares 1992).

11. Max Weber (1972) observes that "many Chinese have been brought up in the Confucian ethic . . . and still consult Taoist diving priests before building a house. . . . Chinese will mourn the deceased relatives according to the Confucian rule while also arranging for Buddhist masses to be performed in their memory" (p. 62).

I met some Japanese Brazilians who declared themselves equally Buddhist and Catholic. The high rate of conversion to Catholicism of Japanese immigrants in Brazil, observed by different researchers, such as Teiiti Suzuki (1969) and J. Mizuki (1978), probably does not imply the rejection of Buddhism by this population.

12. In Brazil this tendency was well described by Carlos R. Brandão (1980), Rubem César Fernandes (1982), Pedro Ribeiro de Oliveira (1975), Cláudio Peranni (1975), and Emile Willems (1967).

13. Several messianic movements occurred in the Brazilian rural area in the last century and the first half of this century. See the studies by Cunha (1940), Facó (1965) and Pereira de Queiroz (1958).

14. For instance, in rural Pernambuco there are lay pilgrimages to the shrine of Santa Quitéria that are not accepted by the Catholic church. In research Marjo De Theije and I did at this shrine, we observed that most pilgrims never noticed that there is no Mass and priests at Santa Quitéria's shrine and celebration day (Mariz and De Theije 1991).

15. Comparing Afro-Brazilian Spiritists with Pentecostals, Peter Fry and Gary Howe (1975) and Eugene Broody observed that the latter tend more often to be recruited among recent rural immigrants.

16. João H. Mendonça (1975) describes the growth of Afro-Spiritism in Recife, northeast of Brazil. He estimates that from 1951 to 1975, the number of Afro-Brazilian religious groups in Recife grew from 120 to 6,000. In São Paulo city the growth rate was even higher; from 1940 to 1980 the Afro-Brazilian Spiritist centers grew from 85 to 19,500 (Prandi

1991). Certainly, the immigration from the Northeast to São Paulo contributes, in part, to this higher growth.

17. In my field research Catholic leaders mentioned the importance of accepting Afro-Brazilian cults. A pastoral agent I interviewed in Recife said, "The liberation theology accepts Afro-Brazilian Spiritism." He referred to the priest of a neighboring parish, who gives a special place to Afro-Brazilian people on the feast day of the Immaculate Conception, in this area identified with Iemanjá (an African *orixá*). I also met a Catholic priest in the neighborhood of Rocha Miranda, Rio de Janeiro, whose parish is devoted to St. Bárbara. After Vatican II, this saint, who is identified with Iança, another African *orixa*, was no longer accepted by the official church. This priest told me that he does not reject devotion to the saint but tries to support it. For instance, he wrote a devotional book on St. Bárbara for his parishioners. He also has tried to be closer to Afro-Brazilian religious leaders and to accept their homage to St. Bárbara in his church.

18. In the different states or regions of the country this type of religion receives specific names. For instance, in Pernambuco it is called Xangô (pronounced "Shango") in Para, Batuque, and in Maranhão, Tambor de Mina. Candomblé, considered by anthropologists to be a generic name, is the term used in Bahia.

19. Nevertheless, the deepening of religious experience in Umbanda may lead the faithful back to Candomblé, as Prandi (1991) shows.

20. According to Waldo César (1973), the Anglican church arrived in Brazil in 1810, the Lutheran in 1823, the Methodist in 1835, the Congregational in 1855, the Presbyterian in 1859, the Baptist in 1882, and the Episcopal in 1890.

21. Antônio Gouvêia Mendonça (1984) analyzes the difficulties accompanying the penetration of historical Protestant churches in Brazil.

22. These kinds of churches are multiplying. Therefore it is very difficult to obtain a complete list of all of them in Brazil.

23. In 1990 they had four churches in the United States, two in Argentina, and one in Uruguay (Oro 1991).

24. See, for instance, Christian Lalive D'Epinay (1969), Judith Hoffnagel (1978), Francisco Cartaxo Rolim (1980, 1985), among others.

25. The Federal Deputy Benedita da Silva is from the Assembly of God and is a member of the Worker party (*Partido dos Trabalhadores*, or PT). In 1992 she was a candidate for mayor of Rio de Janeiro (see Chapter 5). Abumanssur (1987) describes another example of a Pentecostal pastor who is a leader of a neighborhood association and does not hold a conservative orientation.

26. Some of my interviewees refer to the high degree of institutionalization of the Assembly of God of Brazil. Nowadays, this church in Rio de Janeiro is using a computer system. It also publishes several journals: *O Mensageiro* and *Seara* are two of them. According to one of the interviewees, the circulation of *O Mensageiro* is 1.1 million. The interviewee also mentioned that 5,000 members of the Assembly of God participated in its convention in 1987. In this convention some leaders tried to discuss liberation theology. A pastor from the Methodist church suggests that the Brazilian Assembly of God can now be considered a historical Protestant church.

27. TV RIO Canal 13 is a Protestant television station. It is not exclusively controlled by Pentecostals, but Pentecostals are very influential at the station.

Chapter II

1. Amartya Sen (1978, 1981) discusses and assesses the different approaches and methods used to identify the poor and measure their poverty. Sen (1978) explains the "income method": "The first step is to calculate the minimum income P at which all specified needs are satisfied. The next step is to identify those whose actual incomes fall below that line P" (p. 19).

2. As Susan Eckstein (1977) remarked in relation to Mexico.

3. In 1988, 26.2 percent of the total Brazilian population earned one-fourth the minimum wage 1980 per capita, whereas in Northeast Brazil this category comprised 51.2 percent. Life expectancy in Brazil as a whole in 1988 was sixty-five years; in the Northeast, it was fifty-five (Valle Silva 1991).

4. Jaguaribe et al.'s (1986) data also show the inequality between gender. There are more poor women than poor men; 57 percent of the male working population and 67.5 percent of the female earn two minimum wages or less in Brazil.

5. Jaguaribe et al.'s (1986) data seem to contradict Pastore's (1982) study about social mobility in Brazil. In his study Pastore says that the rate of intergenerational upward mobility in Brazil in the 1970s was 57 percent. He identifies social mobility with occupational mobility. I also observed intergenerational occupational mobility among my interviewees; however, I noted that this change in type of occupations did not imply a substantial increase in income. This can be explained by the decrease in wages, or so-called *achatamento salarial* (salarial flattening) described by Faria (1983). Most of the people who have higher occupations than their parents still earn less than two minimum wages. Perhaps the remuneration of many occupations in Brazil has decreased with the multiplication of their positions during the 1960s and 1970s.

6. These authors, such as Emile Willems (1967), Roger Bastide (1960), William Read et al. (1969), and D. L. Clawson (1984), have not focused on Pentecostals. They have tended to consider Pentecostalism to be simply a type of Protestantism. In contrast, Willems (1967) believed that Pentecostals would not make the same degree of economic progress as would Protestants from other denominations.

7. In order to go to college in Brazil a large amount of money is not necessary because there are several public universities.

8. But in an earlier study in the Rio de Janeiro metropolitan area Francisco Rolim (1980) observed a higher proportion of employed people in the CEB he researched.

9. The data about the level of instruction of people at this meeting show that 6 percent never went to school; 12 percent entered the *Primário* but did not finish it "first degree" (which means they had less than four years of schooling); 14 percent finished the *Primário* (four or five years of schooling); 24 percent entered the *Ginásio* (between five and nine years of schooling); 30 percent attended the *Segundo Grau* (between nine and thirteen years of schooling); and 14 percent went on to college. It is important to note that these data include priests and nuns. These people may constitute half of those who have a college degree.

10. A telephone in Brazil is an expensive acquisition. It is an exclusive commodity for members of the middle and upper classes.

11. My data refers only to single women. I did not find any single man heading a family.

12. Ruth Sidel (1986) observes the same fact among the poor in the United States.

13. I use this term in the sense of David Maybury-Lewis's article "Estrutura e Estratégias" (1987). Maybury-Lewis (1988) discusses the relationship between structure and strategies and stresses the importance of an interpretation of social reality that integrates both levels of analysis.

Chapter III

1. I use the expressions "folk Catholicism" and sometimes "folk religion," but I am aware that they may not be the best terms. As Lancaster (1987b) reminds us, Redfield's classic use of the term "folk" refers to a rural tradition in opposition to an urban worldview. The religious phenomenon I am dealing with is not exclusively rural at all; in fact, most of my data refer to urban dwellers. Moreover, this rural–urban opposition is not helpful in understanding the current Brazilian reality (Leeds and Leeds 1970). Therefore I do not use "folk" as Redfield did and use the expression "popular religion" to refer to the same phenomenon. My concept of popular religion is similar to Cook's (1985).

2. Benedetti (1988) and Gómez de Souza (1989) note the differences between CEB members' view and those of pastoral agents.

3. Interview with Pastor Walter Brunelli from the Assembly of God, São Paulo.

4. Both religious groups are developing a "reform" of popular culture in Brazil. When Brazilian Pentecostals identify Afro-Brazilian spiritual entities as the devil, they are carrying on a "reform" similar to that made by Catholic and Protestant churches in Europe in the 15th and 16th centuries, described by Peter Burke (1989).

5. This is the most common pattern in the Assembly of God and other Pentecostal churches in Brazil. But as I mentioned in Chapter 1, the Assembly of God is changing, and some Assembly of God pastors, especially in southeastern Brazil, are

adopting the values and ideas of historical Protestantism. I interviewed an Assembly of God pastor from São Paulo who used, in his interview, the concept of popular culture; he made the distinction between doctrine and cultural habits very clear. His church was in a middle-class neighborhood in São Paulo, and among his church members were physicians and other middle-class professionals. He also told me that these people were mostly new converts and were not from poor Pentecostal families.

6. Reports on the Sixth National Interecclesiastic Meeting of CEBs in 1986 in Trindade, Goias, describe the attempt of doing so by re-creating rituals.

7. Yet Pentecostal churches do adopt new symbols, for instance, the Bible and blessed oil.

8. For instance, see Libânio's (1986) description of the Sixth Interecclesiastical Meeting of CEBs.

9. Friar Betto (1984) affirms that the linear conception of history is a Judeo-Christian revelation.

10. In Afro-Brazilian religions people must obey their *orixá*'s rules, which are not ethical. For instance, a woman whose *orixá* is Iemanja cannot have her hair cut. Umbanda is more ethical.

11. From *Lições Bíblicas*, textbook of the Assembly of God's Sunday school.

12. See, for instance, the booklet of the Campanha da Fraternidade (1988) by the CEBs of Recife.

13. I am referring to larger denominations, such as the *Assembléia de Deus* and *Congregação Cristã do Brasil*. But I do not deny the important role of personal charisma in Pentecostal churches. Some churches seem to be owned by their religious leaders, whose authority is personality based (or charismatically legitimated). This is true of the *Igreja Universal do Reino de Deus*, whose founder and main leader is the controversial Bishop Macedo. For other examples, see Aubrée (1984), Page (1984), and Raphael (1975).

14. But the *Igreja Universal do Reino de Deus*, the Pentecostal church that has grown most in the past few years in Brazil, is almost the private property of Bishop Macedo (Rubim 1990).

15. See, for instance, Aubrée (1984), Bobsin (1984), Gomes (1985), Hoffnagel (1975), Rolim (1985).

16. Zaluar (1985) stresses the authoritarian practices of popular culture. I observed this practice in the description of the internal politics of Carnival clubs in Pernambuco.

17. Santos (1986) describes rites of initiation in Candomblé. Umbanda does not require the same rites.

Chapter IV

1. According to Reginaldo Prandi (1991) this ritual (*jogo de búzios*) is a characteristic of Candomblé and is not present in Umbanda. Candomblé people believe that they may discover people's personalities, problems, and future through the analysis of shells, or *búzios*. Therefore Graças and Luís, who identified themselves as Spiritists, seem to practice Xangô, but a kind of Xangô Umbandizado, as Motta (1992) would say.

2. John Page (1984) presents an extensive review of this literature.

3. See examples in the studies by Regina Novaes (1985), Bryan Roberts (1968), Francisco Rolim (1980), and Beatriz de Muniz de Souza (1969), among others.

Chapter V

1. For instance, see Adriance (1986), Bruneau (1982), Della Cava (1986), Dodson and Montgomery (1982), Epinay (1969), Glazier (1980), Hewitt (1988), Lancaster (1987a, 1987b), Levine (1985, 1986, 1988), Mainwaring (1987), and Viola and Mainwaring (1987), among others.

2. Alba Zaluar (1985) discusses the limits of the "clientele" exchanges of votes for favors. The increase in the number of voters made it impossible to attend to all demands.

3. Willem Assies (1992), Maria do Céu Cézar (1985), and Alexandrina Moura (1988) describe the history and role of the residents' association in Recife.

4. *Orixá* (pronounced "orisha") is a spiritual entity in the African tradition sometimes identified with Catholic saints.

5. Amália P. Barreto (1989) remarks that this prejudice has decreased, especially in Rio de Janeiro, but I felt this prejudice among many interviewees, and some Afro-Brazilian Spiritists

explained that they needed to be discreet in expressing their beliefs.

6. Zaluar (1985) also observes the high value to authoritarian leaders. A very admired president of the Bonsucesso Futebol Clube of Alto José do Pinho, Recife was known as the *presidente de ferro* (the iron president).

7. See for instance, Judith Hoffnagel (1978), Regina Novaes (1985), and Sandra Stoll (1986), among others.

8. Paul Freston (1989) studies the growing number of Protestant deputies in the Brazilian National Congress.

9. For instance, Aubrée (1984), Hoffnagel (1978), and Rolim (1985), among others.

10. See, for instance, Madeleine Adriance (1986), Luiza Fernandes (1985), and Carmem Macedo (1986), among others. Adriance (1986) and Mainwaring (1986) offer a good historical description of this process in the Brazilian Catholic church. They also point out the importance of CEBs within the political proposals of progressive Catholicism in Brazil.

11. See, among others, Gustavo Castro (1987) and Carmem Macedo (1986) in Brazil, Daniel Levine (1988) in Colombia, and Gabriela Valdes Villalva (1988) in Mexico.

Chapter VI

1. See, for instance, Epinay (1969), who analyzed Chilean Pentecostals, and Flora (1976), who studied Pentecostals in Colombia.

2. Epinay (1969) observes the same in Chile, but I disagree with his interpretation that this fact indicates a Pentecostal otherworldliness.

3. For this reason, I underscore the utility of Pentecostal passivity criticized by Aubrée (1984).

4. As Moura (1988) shows, "in Brazil, land invasion constitutes an informal mechanism of access to urban land." People occupy public or private areas without holding title of property. "Squatting is a daily strategy of survival by low income strata" (p. 30).

5. In this respect, my data agree with those of Hoffnagel (1978), Tennekes (1985) and Flora (1976).

6. According to Weber (1958, 72), when capitalism is already established in a society, people do not need any more religious motivation to engage in it. Those who do not follow the "spirit of capitalism" will be punished by economic failure.

7. I met only one CEB member who declared that he was not religious before joining this group. Most people were already practicing Catholics before becoming CEB members. Nevertheless, most mentioned a change. Ernestina, for instance, said, "I used to live in the church, but I did not know what was happening there." Aniceto and Margarida also made similar declarations.

8. Other researchers, such as Duarte (1983) and Giancarlo Petrini (1984), also mention CEB members who experienced a transformation and a "discovery" in their lives after their engagement in these religious activities.

9. Willems (1967) refers to this fact. See, for instance, the description by Cunha (1940) of the religious movement of Canudos.

10. Juana E. dos Santos (1986) mentions some practices and items of knowledge that are exclusive to the leaders of Afro-Brazilian Spiritism. Reginaldo Prandi (1991) and Marion Aubrée (1984) note that the doctrine of this religion depends largely on specific leaders.

11. I also observed this use of respectful titles at the *associação de moradores* (residents' association) meeting in Alto José do Pinho. The members addressed each other with titles such as *Nobre Presidente Dona Zefinha* (Noble President Dona Zefinha), and *Nobre Tesoureiro* (Noble Treasurer). Zaluar (1985) also observed the value of respect among the poor people in Rio de Janeiro.

12. See, for instance, Bobsin (1984), Novaes (1985), and Rolim (1985).

13. Examples of criticism of this morality are found in Marion Aubrée (1984) and Eliane Gouveia (1987).

14. Helenilda Cavalcanti (1985) identifies this kind of experience among the very poor of Recife and discusses the literature on the psychology of poverty, which describes the effect of this experience.

15. Kessel and Guerrero (1987) describe how the success of a mis-

sionary pastor was related to some cures. The conversion of
D. Taso, described by Mintz (1960), also occurred through
healing.

16. Hurbon (1986) observes that in Jamaica many people were
attracted to the Jehovah's Witnesses or Seventh Day Adventist churches because these churches offered protection from
black magic.

17. Weber (1972) affirms: "There is the very important factor of
liberation from fear of noxious spirits and bad magic of any
sort, which is held to be responsible for the majority of all
evils in life. That Christ broke the power of the demons by the
force of his spirit and redeemed his followers from their control, was in the early period of Christianity, one of the most
important and influential of its messages" (p. 148).

18. According to Weber (1972): "Belief in providence is the consistent rationalization of magical divination, to which it is
related, and which for that very reason it seeks to devaluate
as completely as possible, as a matter of principle. No other
view of the religious relationship could possibly be as radically
opposed to all magic, both in theory and in practice, as this
belief in providence which was dominant in the great theistic
religions of Asia Minor and the Occident" (p. 143).

19. The situation of some poor people in Brazil (especially during
the present economic crisis) may be compared with the situation of a prisoner. The poor people's total lack of resources results in very limited opportunities to choose, very limited free-
dom. The similarity between the experience of a prisoner and
an extremely poor person was pointed out by an inhabitant of
a slum in Recife who was interviewed by Cavalcanti (1975).

20. In this analysis, both Weber's and Durkheim's interpretations
are useful in understanding the role religion plays among the
Brazilian poor.

REFERENCES

Abumanssur, E. 1987. "Pentecostais e Trabalho Comunitário." *Comunicações do ISER* 6:(24).

Adriance, M. 1986. *Opting for the Poor: The Brazilian Catholicism in Transition.* Kansas City: Sheed and Ward.

Aguiar, R. O. 1978. *O Ideal Mediúnico.* Recife: Editora Massangana.

Anderson, R. M. 1979. *Vision of the Disinherited: The Making of American Pentecostalism.* New York: Oxford University Press.

Antoniazzi, A. 1989. "O catolicismo no Brasil." In L. Landin, ed., *Sinais do Tempo; Tradições Religiosas no Brasil* Vol. 1. Cadernos do ISER, No. 22. Rio de Janeiro: ISER.

Antonovsky, A. 1979. *Health, Stress and Coping.* San Francisco: Jossey Bass.

Arquidiocese de Goiânia. 1986. "CEB's, Povo de Deus em Busca da Terra Prometida." *Revista da Arquidiocese* 29, nos. 7–9.

Assies, W. 1992. *To Get Out of the Mud: Neighborhood Associativism in Recife. 1964–1988.* Amsterdam: CEDLA.

Aubrée, M. J. 1984. "Voyages entre Corps et Esprits: Étude Comparative entre Deux Courants Religieuses dans le Nordest Brésilien." Third cycle doctoral dissertation, University of Paris.

Azzi, R. 1991. "As Romarias de Juazeiro: Catolicismo Luso-Brasileiro Versus Catolicismo Romanizado." *Revista Eclesiástica Brasileira* 51(202):332–52.

Barreto, M. A. 1989. "Cultos Afro-Brasileiros; O Problema da Clientela." In L. Landim, ed., *Sinais do Tempo; Tradições Religiosas no Brasil.* Vol. 1. Cadernos do ISER, No. 22. Rio de Janeiro: ISER.

Bastide, R. 1960. *Les Réligions Afro-Brèsiliennes: Contribuction à une Sociologie des Interpenetrations de Civilisations.* Paris: Presses Universitaires de France.

Benedetti, L. R. 1988. "Templo, Praça, Coração." Doctoral dissertation, University of São Paulo.

Berger, P. L. 1963. *Invitation to Sociology: A Humanistic Perspective.* New York: Doubleday.

——. 1969. *The Sacred Canopy: Elements of a Sociological Theory of Religion.* New York: Doubleday.

——. 1974. *Pyramids of Sacrifice: Political Ethics and Social Change.* Garden City, N.Y.: Doubleday.

Berger, P. L., B. Berger, and H. Kellner. 1973. *The Homeless Mind: Modernization and Consciousness.* New York: Vintage Books.

Berger, P. L., and T. Luckmann. 1966. *The Social Construction of Reality.* Garden City, N.Y.: Doubleday.

Betto, Frei. 1984. *O que é Comunidade Eclesial de Base.* 5th ed. São Paulo: Brasiliense.

Birman, P. 1983. *O que é Umbanda.* São Paulo: Brasiliense.

——. 1985. "Registrado em Cartório com Firma Reconhecida: A Mediação Política das Federações de Umbanda." In *Umbanda & Política.* Cadernos do ISER, No. 18. Rio de Janeiro: ISER/Marco Zero.

Bobsin, O. 1984. "Produção Religiosa e Significação Social do Pentecostalismo a Partir de sua Prática e Representação." Master's dissertation, Pontifical Catholic University of São Paulo.

Bourdieu, P. 1971. "Génese et Structure du Champ Religieux." *Revue Française de sociologie* 12:295–334.

Brandão, C. R. 1980. *Os Deuses do Povo.* São Paulo: Brasiliense.

Brandão, M. C. 1987. "Xangôs Tradicionais e Umbandizados." Doctoral dissertation, University of São Paulo.

Broody, E. B. 1973. *The Lost Ones.* New York: International University Press.

Brown, D. G. 1986. *Umbanda Religion and Politics in Urban Brazil.* Ann Arbor, Mich.: UMI Research Press.

Bruneau, T. 1982. *The Church in Brazil: The Politics of Religion.* Austin: University of Texas Press.

Burdick, J. S. 1989. "Gossip and Secrecy: Women's Articulation of Domestic Conflicts in Three Religions in Urban Brazil." *Sociological Analysis,* 51(2).

——. 1990. "Looking for God in Brazil: The Progressive Catholic Church in Urban Brazil's Religious Arena." Ph.D. dissertation, CUNY.

Burke, P. 1989. *Cultura Popular na Idade Moderna*. São Paulo: Companhia das Letras.

Cabral da Silva, M. G. 1988. "Recentes Teodicéias Inspiradas na Tradição Oriental: Conservadorismo ou Mudança Social?" Master's thesis, Federal University of Pernambuco, Recife.

Cardoso, R. 1978. "Sociedade e Poder: As Representações dos Favelados em São Paulo." *Ensaios de Opinião*, 6:38–44.

———. 1983. "Movimentos Sociais Urbanos: Balanço Crítico." In S. Sorj and M. H. Tavares, eds., *Sociedade e Política no Brasil pós-64*. São Paulo: Brasiliense.

Carneiro, L. P., and L. E. Soares. 1992. "Religiosidade, Estrutura Social e Comportamento Político." In M.C.L. Bingemer, ed., *O impacto da modernidade sobre a religião*. São Paulo: Edições Loyola.

Castro, G. P. 1987. *As Comunidades do Dom: Um Estudo de CEBs no Recife*. Recife: Massangana.

Cavalcanti, H. 1985. "Síndrome da Falta de Poder." *Cadernos de Estudos Sociais*, 1(2):141–60.

Centro Ecumênico de Documentação e Informação (CEDI). 1989. *Povo de Deus na América Latina a Caminho da Libertação; dossiê do Sétimo Encontro Intereclesial de Comunidades de Base (CEBs)*. Rio de Janeiro: CEDI.

César, W. 1973. *Para uma Sociologia do Protestantismo Brasileiro*. Petrópolis: Vozes.

———. 1974. "Urbanização e Religiosidade Popular: Um Estudo da Função da Doutrina Pentecostal na Sociedade Urbana." *Revista de Cultura Vozes*, 8(7):523–32.

Cézar, M. do C. 1985. "As Organizações Populares do Recife: Trajetória e Articulação Política (1955–64)." *Cadernos de Estudos Sociais*, 1(2):161–82.

Clark, C. 1988. *O Urubu e o Boi: A Fome da Burguesia e o Poder Popular*. Recife: FUNDAJ–Depto de Economia.

Clawson, D. 1984. "Religious Allegiance and Development in Rural Latin America." *Journal of Interamerican Studies and World Affairs* 24:499–525.

Clearly, E. L. 1985. *Crisis and Change: The Church in Latin America Today*. Maryknoll, N.Y.: Orbis Books.

Comblim, J. 1983. "Os 'Movimentos' e a Pastoral Latino-americana." *Revista Eclesiástica Brasileira* 4 (fasc. 170).

———. 1987. "Os Leigos." *Comunicações do ISER*, 6(26).

Cook, G. 1985. *The Expectation of the Poor*. Maryknoll, N.Y.: Orbis Books.

Coral-Prieto, L. 1980. *Las Iglesias Evangélicas de Guatemala*. Department of Theology, University Francisco Marroquim.

Cunha, E. da. 1940. *Os Sertões; Campanha de Canudos*. 15th ed. Rio de Janeiro: Francisco Alves.

Curry, D. 1980. "Messianism and Protestantism in Brazil's Sertão." *Journal of Interamerican Studies and World Affairs* 12:461–38.

Da Matta, R. 1983. *Carnaval, Malandros e Heróis*. 4th ed. Rio de Janeiro: Zahar.

Dantas, B. G. 1982. "Repensando a Pureza Nagô." *Religião e Sociedade* 8:15–20.

———. 1988. *Vovô Nagô e Papai Branco; Usos e Abusos da África no Brasil*. Rio de Janeiro: Graal.

Daudelin, J. 1991. "Brazil's Progressive Church in Crisis: Institutional Weakness and Political Vulnerability." Manuscript.

Della-Cava, R. 1970. *Miracle at Joazeiro*. New York: Columbia University Press.

———. 1986. "A Igreja e a Abertura 1974–1985." In P. Krischke and S. Mainwaring, eds., *A Igreja nas Bases em Tempo de Transição*. Porto Alegre: L&PM/CEDEC.

Denton, C. F. 1971. "Protestantism and Latin America Middle-Class." *Practical Anthropology* 18:24–28.

De Theije, M. 1990. "'Brotherhoods Throw More Weight Around than the Pope': Catholic Traditionalism and the Lay Brotherhoods of Brazil," *Sociological Analysis* 52(2):189–204.

Dodson, M., and T. W. Montgomery. 1982. "The Churches in the Nicaragua Revolution." In T. W. Walker, ed., *Nicaragua in Revolution*. New York: Praeger.

Duarte, L.M.S. 1983. *Isto não se Aprende na Escola: A Educação do Povo nas CEBs*. Petrópolis: Vozes.

Durham, E., and R. Cardoso. 1977. "Elaboração Cultural e Participação Social nas Populações de Baixa Renda." *Ciência e Cultura* 29(2):171–77.

Eckstein, S. 1977. *The Poverty of Revolution*. Princeton: Princeton University Press.

Epinay, C.L.D. 1969. *Haven to the Masses: A Study of the Pentecostal Movement in Chile*. London: Lutterworth Press.

Facó, R. 1965. *Cangaceiros e Fanáticos*. Rio de Janeiro: Civilização Brasileira.

Faria, V. 1983. "Desenvolvimento, Urbanização e Mudanças na Estrutura do Emprego: A Experiência Brasileira dos Últimos Anos." In B. Sorj and M. H. Tavares, eds., *Sociedade e Política no Brasil pós-64*. São Paulo: Brasiliense.

————. 1991. "A Conjuntura Social Brasileira: Dilemas e Perspectivas." *Cadernos de Conjuntura* 42:21–44. Rio: IUPERJ.

Fernandes, L.B.A. 1985. "The Contribution of Basic Ecclesial Communities to an Education for Social Transformation in Brazil." Ph.D. dissertation, Harvard Graduate School of Education.

Fernandes, R. C. 1982. *Os Cavaleiros do Bom Jesus*. São Paulo: Brasiliense.

————. 1992. Censo Institucional Evangélico CIN 1992: Comentários. Rio de Janeiro: ISER.

Flora, C. 1976. *Pentecostalism in Colombia: Baptism by Fire and Spirit*. Cranbury, N.J.: Fairleigh Dickson University Press.

Floriano, M. G., and R. Novaes 1985. "O Negro Evangélico." *Comunicações do ISER* 4. Edição Especial.

Freston, P. 1989. "Teocratas, Fisiológicos Nova Direita e Progressistas: Protestantes e Política na Nova República." Paper presented at Twelfth ANPOCS, Caxambu.

Fry, P., and G. Howe. 1975. "Duas Respostas à Aflição: Umbanda e Pentecostalismo." *Debate e Crítica* 6:75–94.

Fundação Instituto "Brasileiro de Geografia e Estatística–IBGE." 1982. *IX Recenseamento Geral do Brasil 1980–Censo Demográfico*. Rio de Janeiro: IBGE.

————. 1990. *Participação Político-social, 1988: Brasil e Grandes Regiões*. Vol. 3. Rio de Janeiro: IBGE.

Geertz, C. 1975. *The Interpretation of Culture*. New York: Basis Books.

Geiger, L. I. 1992. "A Ambivalência da Pastoral Popular Libertadora Frente à Razão Moderna." Paper presented at Sixteenth ANPOCS, Caxambu.

Gilkes, C. T. 1985. "Together and in Harness: Women's Tradition in the Sanctified Church." *Signs: Journal of Women in Culture and Society* 10:678–99.

Glazier, S., ed. 1980. *Pentecostalism: Case Studies in Latin America and Caribee*. St. Louis: Washington University Press.

Gomes, J. F. 1985. "Religião e Política: Os Pentecostais no Recife." Master's thesis, Federal University of Pernambuco, Recife.

Gómez de Souza, L. A. 1989. "Sinais dos Tempos: Transformações Recentes no Campo Religioso Brasileiro." In L. Landim, ed., *Sinais do Tempo; Tradições Religiosas no Brasil*. Vol. 1 Cadernos do ISER, No. 22. Rio de Janeiro: ISER.

Gouveia, E. M. 1987. "O Silêncio que deve ser ouvido Mulheres Pentecostais em São Paulo." Master's thesis, Pontifical Catholic University of São Paulo.

Gregory, A. 1973. *Comunidades Eclesiais de Base: Utopia ou Realidade*. Rio de Janeiro: Vozes/CERIS.

Guimarães, E.A.M. 1992. "Catolicismo Popular e Afro-Brasilidade na Festa do Bonfim." Paper presented at the Associação Brasileira de Antropologia (ABA) annual meeting.

Harris, M. 1956. *Town and Country in Brazil*. New York: Columbia University Press.

Hewitt, E. W. 1986. "Strategies for Social Change Employed by Comunidades Eclesiais de Base (CEBs) in the Archdiocese of São Paulo." *Journal for the Scientific Study of Religion* 25(1):1–139.

———. 1987. "The Influence of Social Class on Activity Preferences of Comunidades Eclesiais de Base (CEBs) in the Archdiocese of São Paulo." *Journal of Latin American Studies* 19:141–56.

———. 1988. "Religion and the Consolidation of Democracy in Brazil: The Role of Comunidades Eclesiais de Base (CEBs)." Paper presented at the SSSR Conference, Chicago.

Hoffnagel, J. C. 1978. "The Believers: Pentecostalism in a Brazilian City." Ph.D. dissertation, Indiana University.

Hoornaert, E. 1988. "As Comunidades Eclesiais de Base no Brasil: Entre a Ortodoxia e a Heresia." Paper presented at 46th International Conference of Americanists, Amsterdam.

Hunter, J. 1989. "Theory on Fundamentalism." Paper presented to the Sociology Department of Boston University, Boston.

Hurbon, L. 1986. "New Religious Movements in the Caribbean." In J. Beckford, ed., *New Religious Movements and Rapid Social Change*. London: Sage/UNESCO.

Ireland, R. 1986. "Comunidades Eclesiais de Base, Grupos Espíri-

tas e a Democratização no Brasil." In P. Krischke and
G. Mainwaring, eds., *A Igreja nas Bases em Tempos de Transição*. Porto Alegre: L&PM-CEDEC.

Jacobi, P. R. 1987. "Movimentos Sociais: Teoria e Prática em
Questão." In I. Sherer-Warren and P. J. Krischke, eds.,
*Uma Revolução no Cotidiano: Os Novos Movimentos Sociais
na América do Sul*. São Paulo: Brasiliense.

Jaguaribe, H., W. Santos, M. Paiva de Abreu, W. Fritsch, and
F. Bastos de Avila. 1986. *Brasil, 2000; Para um Pacto
Social*. Rio de Janeiro: Paz e Terra.

Jaguaribe, H., N. Valle Silva, M. Paiva de Abreu, F. Bastos de
Avila, and W. Fritsch 1989. *Brasil: Reforma ou Caos*, Rio
de Janeiro: Paz e Terra.

Jatobá, J. 1988. "Pobreza Urbana, Mercados de Trabalho e Desenvolvimento Regional: O Caso do Brasil." Paper presented
at 46th International Conference of Americanists, Amsterdam.

Kadt, E. 1967. "The Church and Social Change in Brazil." In
C. Veliz, ed., *The Politics of Conformity in Latin America*.
London: Oxford University Press.

Kessel, J., and B. Guerrero. 1987. "Sanidad y Salvación en el Alti-
plano Chileno; Del Yatiri al Pastor." *Cuaderno de Investigación Social* 3:21.

Kloppenburgo, B. 1960. *O Espiritismo no Brasil*. Petrópolis: Vozes.

Lancaster, R. N. 1987a. "Popular Religion and Class Consciousness in Managua's Working Class Barrios." Paper presented at the American Ethnological Society Conference,
San Antonio.

————. 1987b. "Thanks to God and the Revolution: Popular Religion and Class Consciousness in the New Nicaragua."
Ph.D. dissertation, University of California, Berkeley.

Leacock, E. B. 1971. *The Culture of Poverty: A Critique*. New York:
Simon and Schuster.

Leeds, A. 1964. "Brazilian Careers and Social Structure: A
Case History and Model in Contemporary Cultures
and Society in Latin America." *American Anthropologist*
66:1321–47.

————. 1971. "The Concept of the 'Culture of Poverty': Concep-
tual, Logical and Empirical Problems, with Perspectives
from Brazil and Peru." In E. B. Leacock, ed., *The Culture*

of Poverty: A Critique. New York: Simon and Schuster.

Leeds, A., and E. Leeds 1970. "Brazil and the Myth of Urban Rurality: Urban Experience, Work and Values in 'Squatments' of Rio de Janeiro and Lima." In A. J. Field, ed., *City and Country in the Third World; Issues of Modernization of Latin America.* Cambridge, Mass.: Schenkman.

Leonard, E. 1969. *O Protestantismo Brasileiro: Estudo de Eclesiologia e História Social.* São Paulo: Aste.

Levine, D. 1985. "Religion and Politics: Drawing Lines, Understanding Changes." *Latin American Research Review* 20(1):7–25.

——, ed. 1986. *Religion and Political Conflict in Latin America.* Chapel Hill: University of North Carolina Press.

——. 1988. "Popular Groups and Popular Culture." Paper presented at the SSSR Conference, Chicago.

Libânio, J. B. 1986. "CEBs: Igreja em Busca da Terra Prometida." *Revista Eclesiástica Brasileira* 46(183):489–511.

Lima, D. M. de 1988. *Os Demônios Descem do Norte.* Rio de Janeiro: Francisco Alves.

Love, J. 1970. "Political Participation in Brazil 1881–1964." *Luso-Brazilian Review* 7(2):1–24.

Macedo, C. C. 1986. *Tempo de Gênesis: O Povo das Comunidades Eclesiais de Base.* São Paulo: Brasiliense.

Mainwaring, S. 1986. *The Catholic Church and Politics in Brazil: 1916–1985.* Stanford, Calif.: Stanford University Press.

Mariz, C. L. 1990. "Pentacostalismo y Alcoholismo entre los Pobres del Brasil." *Cristianismo y Sociedad* 105:39–44.

——. 1992. "As igrejas Pentecostais e a Recuperação do Alcoolismo." Paper presented at the 44th SBPC, São Paulo.

Mariz, C. L. and Marjo De Theije 1991. "A Santa do Povo: O Catolicismo dos Leigos no Santuário de Santa Quitéria." *Comunicações do ISER* 10(41):42–57.

Martin, D. 1990. *Tongues of Fire: The Explosion of Protestantism in Latin American,* Oxford: Blackwell.

Marx, K. 1957. *On Religion.* Moscow: Foreign Languages Publishing.

Maués, H. 1987. "A Tensão Constitutiva do Catolicismo Popular e o Controle Eclesiástico." Doctoral dissertation, National Museum–Federal University of Rio de Janeiro.

Maybury-Lewis, D. 1988. "Estruturas e Estratégias." *Anuário*

Antropológico 86. Brasília: Universidade de Brasília/Tempo Brasileiro.

Medeiros, B.T.F. de. 1988. "O Sincretismo Católico Afro-Brasileiro numa Festa de Padroeira: Um Estudo de Caso." Paper presented at the 46th International Conference of Americanists, Amsterdam.

——. 1991. "Oxalá-Jesus: Fotos, Entrevistas e Videoteipes." *Comunicações do ISER* 10(41):75–88.

Mendonça, A. G. 1984. *O Celeste Povir; A Inserção do Protestantismo no Brasil*. São Paulo: Paulinas.

Mendonça, A. G. and P. Velasques. 1990. *Introdução ao Protestantismo no Brasil*. São Paulo: Loyola.

Mendonça, J. H. 1975. "O Crescimento dos Centros e Terreiros de Xangô no Grande Recife." *Ciência e Trópico* 3(1):41–63.

Mintz, S. 1960. *Worker in the Cane: A Puerto Rican Life History*. Westport, Conn.: Greenwood Press.

Mizuki, J. 1978. *The Growth of the Japanese Church in Brazil*. South Pasadena, Calif.: William Carey Library.

Motta, R. 1977. "Renda, Emprego, Nutrição e Religião." *Ciência e Trópico* 5(2):129–39.

——. 1983. "Meat and Feast: The Xangô Religion in Recife, Brazil." Ph.D. dissertation, Columbia University.

——. 1988. "A Eclesificação dos Cultos Afro-Brasileiros." *Comunicações do ISER* 7(30):31–43.

——. 1992. "Edjé Balé; Alguns Aspectos do Sacrifício no Xangô de Pernambuco." Titular Professor's thesis, Federal University of Pernambuco, Recife.

Moura, A. S. 1988. "State and Unofficial Housing Production in Brazil." Paper presented at the 46th International Conference of Americanists, Amsterdam.

Niemayer, A. M. 1979. "Favela: 'Iguais e Desiguais.'" *Revista de Antropologia* 22:113–31.

Novaes, R. 1984. "Mutirões, Cooperativas e Roças Comunitárias." In N. Esterci, ed., *Cooperativismo e Coletivização no Campo*. Rio de Janeiro: ISER/Marco Zero.

——. 1985. *Os Escolhidos de Deus*. Cadernos do ISER, No. 19. Rio de Janeiro: ISER/Marco Zero.

Oliveira, P. R. 1975. "Catolicismo Popular com Base Religiosa." *Tempo e Presença*. CEI suplemento 12:3–11.

Oro, A. P. 1991. "O Discurso dos Pregadores Eletrônicos." *Cader-*

nos de Antropologia 2:23–37 (published by the Programa de Pós-Graduação em Antropologia Social da Universidade Federal do Rio Grande do Sul).

Ortiz, R. 1974. *A Morte Branca do Feiticeiro Negro.* Petrópolis: Vozes.

Page, J. J. 1984. "Brasil para Cristo: The Cultural Construction of Pentecostals Networks in Brazil." Ph.D. dissertation, New York University.

Pastore, J. 1982. *Inequality and Social Mobility in Brazil.* Madison: University of Wisconsin Press.

Peranni, C. 1975. "Religiosidade Popular e Mudança Social." *Tempo e Presença.* CEI suplemento 12:15–24.

Pereira de Queiroz, M. I. 1958. "Classification des Messianism Brèsiliens." *Archives de Sociologie des Réligions* 5:111–20.

Petrini, G. 1984. "CEBs em São Paulo; um Novo Sujeito Popular." Master's thesis, Pontifícia Universidade Católica de São Paulo.

Pierucci, A. F. de O. 1987. "Origem Sócio-cultural do Clero Católico." Paper presented at the 11th Annual Meeting of ANPOCS, Águas de São Pedro.

Prandi, R. 1988. "Sincretismo Afro-brasileiro em São Paulo: Da Umbanda ao Candomblé." Paper presented at the 46th International Conference of Americanists, Amsterdam.

———. 1991. *Os Candomblés de São Paulo: Velha Magia na Metropóle Nova.* São Paulo: HUCITEC and Editora da Universidade de São Paulo.

Ramalho, J. P. 1977. "Algumas Notas Sobre Duas Perspectivas de Pastoral Popular." *Cadernos do ISER (O Pentecostalismo)* 6:30–37.

Raphael, A. 1975. "Miracles in Brazil: A Study of the Pentecostal Movement 'O Brasil para Cristo.'" Master's thesis, Columbia University.

Read, W., V. Monterroso, and A. Johnson, 1969. *Latin American Church Growth.* Grand Rapids, Mich.: Eerdmans.

Ribeiro, R. 1982. *Antropologia da Religião.* Recife: Massangana.

Roberts, B. 1968. "Protestant Groups and Coping with Urban Life in Guatemala." *American Journal of Sociology* 73:753–67.

Rodrigues, R. Nina 1935. *O Animismo Fetichista dos Negros Baianos.* Rio de Janeiro: Civilização Brasileira.

Rolim, F. C. 1980. *Religião e Classes Populares*. Petrópolis: Vozes.

———. 1985. *Pentecostais no Brasil: Uma Interpretação Sócio-religiosa*. Petrópolis: Vozes.

Rubim, C. 1991. "A teologia da opressão." Master's thesis, State University of Campinas, São Paulo.

Santiago, R.L.L. 1988. "Religião, Classes Sociais e Família; O caso do Pentecostalismo." Social Science Department, Federal University of Pernambuco, Ms.

Santos, J. E. dos. 1986. *Os nagôs e a Morte*. 4th ed. Petrópolis: Vozes.

Scott, R. P. 1988. "Gender, Power and Economics among the Urban Poor: Shifts in Poor Women's Views on the Household." Paper presented at the 46th International Conference of Americanists, Amsterdam.

Sen, A. K. 1978. "Three Notes on the Concept of Poverty." *World Employment Programme Research*, 2–23. Working Paper 65. Geneva: ILO.

———. 1981. "Issues in the Measurement of Poverty." In S. Strom, ed., *Measurement in Public Choice*. London: Macmillan.

Sidel, R. 1986. *Women and Children Last: The Plight of Poor Women in Affluent America*. New York: Penguin.

Silva, F. X. 1987. Comportamento Eleitoral da Comunidade Evangélica do Nordeste: As eleições de 1986. Ms., IPESPE, Recife.

Souza, B. M. 1969. *A Experiência da Salvação: Pentecostais em São Paulo*. São Paulo: Duas Cidades.

Stack, C. 1974. *All Our Kin: Strategies for Survival in a Black Community*. New York: Harper & Row.

Stoll, D. 1990. *Is Latin America Turning Protestant? The Politics of Evangelical Growth*. Berkeley: University of California Press.

Stoll, S. J. 1986. "Púlpito e Palanque: Religião e Política nas Eleições da Grande São Paulo." Master's Thesis, State University of Campinas, São Paulo.

Suzuki, T. 1969. *The Japanese Immigrant in Brazil*. Tokyo: University of Tokyo Press.

Tennekes, H. 1985. *El Movimiento Pentecostal en la Sociedad Chilena*. Iquique, Chile: Publicaciones Ocasionales No. 1, Centro de Investigación de la Realidad del Norte (CIREN).

Thomas, K. 1991. *Religião e o Declínio da Magia; Crenças Populares na Inglaterra séculos XVI e XVII*. São Paulo: Companhia das Letras.

Turner, V. 1975. "Symbolic Studies." *Annual Review of Anthropology* 4:145–61.

Valdes-Villalva, G. 1988. "Women in the Latin American Catholic Church." Paper presented at the SSSR Conference, Chicago.

Valentine, C. A. 1968. *Culture and Poverty: A Critique and Counter-Proposals*. Chicago: University of Chicago Press.

Valle Silva, N. do. 1991. "A Situação Social do Fim da Década Perdida." *Cadernos de Conjuntura* 42:1–20. IUPERJ, Rio.

Viola, E., and S. Mainwaring. 1987. "Novos Movimentos Sociais, Cultura Política e Democracia: Brasil e Argentina." In I. Scherer-Warren and P. Krischke, eds., *Uma Revolução no Cotidiano; Os Novos Movimentos Sociais na América do Sul*. São Paulo: Brasiliense.

Weber, M. 1948. "The Protestant Sects and the Spirit of Capitalism." In H. Gerth and C. W. Mills, eds., *From Max Weber: Essays in Sociology*. London: K. Paul, Trench, Trubner.

———. 1958. *The Protestant Ethic and the Spirit of Capitalism*. New York: Scribner's.

———. 1972. *The Sociology of Religion*. 6th ed. Boston: Beacon Press.

Willems, E. 1967. *Followers of New Faith: Culture Change and the Rise of Protestantism in Brazil and Chile*. Nashville: Vanderbilt University Press.

Zaluar, A. 1985. *A Máquina e a Revolta: As Organizações Populares e o Significado da Pobreza*. São Paulo: Brasiliense.

INDEX